D0469320

THE

HARVARD MEDICAL

SCHOOL GUIDE TO

LOWERING YOUR

CHOLESTEROL

MASON W. FREEMAN, M.D.

WITH CHRISTINE JUNGE

McGraw·Hill

New York   Chicago   San Francisco   Lisbon   London   Madrid   Mexico City
Milan   New Delhi   San Juan   Seoul   Singapore   Sydney   Toronto

Library of Congress Cataloging-in-Publication Data

Freeman, Mason W.
    The Harvard Medical School guide to lowering your cholesterol / by Mason W.
Freeman, with Christine Junge.
        p.   cm.
    Includes index.
    ISBN 0-07-144481-5
    1. Hypercholesteremia—Popular works.   2. Coronary heart disease—Prevention—
Popular works.   I. Title: Guide to lowering your cholesterol.   II. Junge, Christine E.
III. Title.

RC632.H83F745   2005
616.1′2305—dc22   2004022729

1 2 3 4 5 6 7 8 9 0   DOC/DOC   0 9 8 7 6 5

ISBN 0-07-144481-5

Interior design by Think Design Group, LLC
Interior artwork by Michael Linkinhoker and Ed Wiederer

McGraw-Hill books are available at special quantity discounts to use as premiums and sales
promotions, or for use in corporate training programs. For more information, please write to
the Director of Special Sales, Professional Publishing, McGraw-Hill, Two Penn Plaza, New York,
NY 10121-2298. Or contact your local bookstore.

The information contained in this book is intended to provide helpful and informative material
on the subject addressed. It is not intended to serve as a replacement for professional
medical advice. Any use of the information in this book is at the reader's discretion. The
author, publisher, and the President and Fellows of Harvard College specifically disclaim any
and all liability arising directly or indirectly from the use or application of any information
contained in this book. A health-care professional should be consulted regarding your specific
situation.

This book is printed on acid-free paper.

This book is dedicated to my mother,
Marion Freeman, late father, Admiral
Mason Freeman, and my wife, Sherry, for
all their love, support, and encouragement.
—Mason

For my parents, Linda and Heinz Junge,
who have been nothing but loving and
supportive from the beginning, and for my
husband, Brian, who has been nothing but
loving and supportive from our beginning.
—Christine

Contents

Preface

What's your cholesterol? It's a question you hear everywhere, from family gatherings to television commercials. Though awareness of the dangers of high cholesterol has greatly increased in the past two decades, there are still many myths out there. The biggest myth, although it is gradually being dispelled, is that all cholesterol is created equal. In reality, as many people are beginning to understand, the cholesterol in our blood is carried in several different particles—the main ones being high-density lipoproteins (HDL) and low-density lipoproteins (LDL). These two types of particles have completely different effects on blood vessels and their likelihood of getting clogged. Put simply, HDL protects your body from heart disease, while LDL can cause it.

That's why Peter and Mary, the patients whose stories are told in this preface, have totally different levels of risk for heart disease, despite having the same total cholesterol level. When you're talking about cholesterol, what matters most isn't your total cholesterol level—it's the breakdown of how that cholesterol is carried. Even individuals with total cholesterol levels below 200—long considered a "safe zone"—can be at high risk for heart disease if they carry too little cholesterol in the HDL particles or have other risk factors that predispose them to the blocked arteries that cause heart attacks.

A Heart Attack at Twenty-Four?

Peter was twenty-four when he first began to experience a heavy pressure in his chest whenever he jogged, split wood, or bicycled up steep hills. He assumed he had pulled a muscle, though he couldn't pinpoint the event that caused this "injury." He tried to ignore the discomfort, but as the weeks went by, the pressure in his chest grew more intense whenever he exercised, and he started to get short of breath with less and less activity. He began to worry that he might have a more serious problem, like the heart disease that had hospitalized his father at forty-four. But Peter was sure that at age twenty-four that couldn't be the explanation.

On a cool, brisk Saturday afternoon, while biking through the autumn foliage in a distant Boston suburb, Peter's pain began again. This time, it did not subside after half an hour, as it had on all the previous occasions. Peter asked a friend on the bike trip to drive him to the local emergency room. Several hours later—after Peter's cardiac catheterization, angioplasty, and stent placement were completed—he found himself wondering what having a heart attack at twenty-four would mean for his business career, his love of aerobic sports, and the young woman he was planning to marry in the spring.

When Peter asked the cardiac care nurse if she could explain how someone so fit and so young could have a heart attack, she said, "Your cholesterol level just came back—it was over 300. I think that explains why you're here."

Three Hundred Is a Healthy Cholesterol Level?

When Mary was sixty-five, her business set up an afternoon health-screening program in the company cafeteria. She got screened during her lunch break and found out that her total cholesterol level was higher than 300. The screeners told her to contact her physician and get advice on treatment. Her family practitioner repeated the test and confirmed the level, asking Mary to try a low-fat, low-cholesterol diet to see if that would improve her numbers. She tried the diet the nutritionist prescribed, faithfully eating the foods on the plan, though she found the meals bland and unappealing.

When she went back to her doctor after two months, her cholesterol level had barely changed. Her doctor advised that she take a cholesterol-lowering pill called a statin. Mary was reluctant to follow this advice. She had never taken any medication before and didn't like the idea of having to take a pill every day. In the back of her mind she heard the voices of several of her friends who were already on cholesterol-lowering pills and who were always complaining about their cost. A few of them even said the medicines had made them feel achy and weak. Mary asked her doctor if she could get a second opinion about the need for treatment.

During her appointment with a specialist, the doctor told her that though her total cholesterol level was above 300, she was not at very high risk for heart disease because her HDL (good) cholesterol was high, while her LDL (bad) cholesterol was low. He made a few simple recommendations about her diet—ones that she knew she could stick with—and encouraged her to get a little more exercise. He said he would write a note to her regular doctor explaining why Mary did not need to take a cholesterol medication.

The Truth About Cholesterol

Another myth about cholesterol is that the healthiest cholesterol level you can have is zero. If people didn't have any cholesterol, they'd die—and so would the human species. Men wouldn't produce testosterone without it, women wouldn't produce estrogen, and without those, humans wouldn't produce the next generation. Your intestines couldn't digest food without cholesterol, and your cells couldn't create their outside coating known as a plasma membrane. So, cholesterol itself isn't bad. What is bad is having too much and carrying it in the LDL particles, which are most prone to depositing it in the wrong places, such as your artery walls.

Most of the cholesterol that travels in your blood is actually made by your liver—only a minority of it comes from cholesterol in the food you eat. Certain fats in your diet besides cholesterol—

particularly saturated fats and trans fats—cause the liver to make unhealthy amounts of cholesterol. Indeed, the saturated fats and trans fats in your diet do more to raise your cholesterol than does the cholesterol in the food you eat.

Regardless of where it comes from, when there's too much LDL in your blood, it gets deposited in the walls of your arteries, the blood vessels that carry oxygen-rich blood to your heart and brain. Through a series of steps we'll discuss in Chapter 2, the accumulation of LDL causes a narrowing and instability in the artery walls, which ultimately can lead to heart attacks and strokes.

The good news is that, for most people, heart disease is preventable if you do heart-healthy things that lower your LDL cholesterol. Lifestyle changes such as eating a diet low in saturated fat and exercising can help you go a long way toward reaching that goal. If they're not enough, there are effective medications to help you. I'll spend the later chapters of the book discussing lifestyle- and medication-based cholesterol control plans and teaching you how to stick with them (the hard part, for some).

This book will also explain everything you need to know about cholesterol on the cellular level, the process for testing your cholesterol and evaluating your results, and how high cholesterol causes problems in the body. In this day and age, no book on cholesterol would be complete without a discussion of holistic approaches, so I spend time dissecting the evidence on the complementary and alternative therapies touted for lowering cholesterol. I also offer advice for specific groups of people, including older adults, people with heart disease, people with diabetes, and children.

All this information comes backed by the latest scientific studies—but simplified so reading and comprehending it isn't a chore. While the science that has led to our understanding of the relationship between cholesterol and heart disease is sometimes complex and technical, the basic concepts underlying the treatment of cholesterol disorders are straightforward and easily understood. I try to avoid using medical jargon when talking to patients in my office, and I avoid doing that in this book.

I will also try to make clear the distinction between what we know with great certainty and what we believe but need more research to confirm. Unfortunately, a lot of medical information is presented to the public as being definitive, when it is anything but, and this leads to a great deal of skepticism when that information is later retracted or contradicted by other studies. After reading this book, you should have better insights into what kinds of medical studies are likely to stand the test of time and which ones are too premature to act on now.

It is important to have a working knowledge of these topics if you are interested in leading a long and healthy life. After all, high cholesterol affects about 18 percent of Americans ages twenty to seventy-four, and atherosclerotic heart disease is the single leading cause of death and disability in the developed world. I am one of the many people who fall into this 18 percent: I saw my cholesterol levels rise in the early 1990s and tried several cholesterol-lowering drugs until I found the one that worked for me. Now, I have my cholesterol under control, but I do battle with a fondness for the same high-fat foods that my patients struggle to cut from their diets. I try to practice what I preach to my patients and recommend in this book, though. I eat a healthy diet and stay active swimming; playing basketball, tennis, and golf; and trying to keep up with my two teenagers, James and Sarah. (I can't, however, keep up with my wife, Sherry Haydock, who is also a doctor and has completed twenty-four marathons.)

My interest in cholesterol emerged much before my own levels rose, and I have my mother to thank for it. In the 1950s, she read about cholesterol and decided to cut butter out of our diet and give me and my siblings only skim milk from then on. She was way ahead of the times on that one, though I distinctly remember not welcoming those changes with much enthusiasm.

I first studied lipoproteins as a medical student at the University of California–San Francisco Medical School and became convinced that cholesterol treatment was critical to the prevention of coronary artery disease. I've devoted my career to it ever since, opening the Lipid Clinic at Massachusetts General Hospital in

1986, where patients with lipid disorders still come from around the world to see me each week. In addition to seeing patients, I direct a research laboratory that has played a key role in identifying and studying proteins that help us understand cholesterol's role in heart disease. This clinical and research work provides the foundation for my thinking about cholesterol disorders. It also provides the knowledge that I try to impart to the young doctors in training at Harvard Medical School, as well as the hundreds of visiting physicians who come to train at Massachusetts General Hospital every year. That experience also forms the basis for this book.

If my years of working with cholesterol have taught me one thing, it's that the link between cholesterol and the risk of heart disease is not a medical fad that's going to disappear from the health-care scene anytime soon. The good news is there's a lot you can do to lower your cholesterol, and every time you lower your LDL cholesterol, your heart disease risk drops substantially. I hope this book will provide the encouragement you need to get your cholesterol under control and keep it there.

Acknowledgments

As with any project of this size, there are many people who worked tirelessly behind the scenes to get this book printed. At Harvard Health Publications, I thank Dr. Tony Komaroff, editor-in-chief, for providing me with the opportunity to publish this book, and for seeing me through the process. Managing Editor Nancy Ferrari edited and provided guidance along the way, and interns Gareth Hughes, Jonah Leshin, and Vered Schreiber helped in innumerable ways. Pat Skerrett and Dr. Thomas Lee, editors of the *Harvard Heart Letter*, also lent much help. Production team Heather Foley, Mary Allen, and Charlene Tiedemann shepherded me through the illustration process, and the illustrations of Michael Linkinhoker and Ed Wiederer beautifully accompany the text. Drs. John G. Byrne, chairman of the Department of Cardiac Surgery at Vanderbilt University, and Donald B. Levy, an instructor of medicine at Harvard Medical School and primary care physician at the Marino Center, lent their expertise to the surgery and alternative medicine sections of the text, respectively. Dr. Kenneth L. Minaker, chief of the geriatric medicine unit at Massachusetts General Hospital and associate professor of medicine at Harvard Medical School, added valuable information to the section on caring for elderly patients.

I would like to thank my coauthor, Christine Junge, who did all the hard work that went into writing the book. Her organizational skills, research diligence, lucid writing, and keen intelligence are evident throughout. What isn't evident is her extraordinary patience and good humor in dealing with a novice author who routinely missed deadlines. Whatever merits a reader finds in the book can be directly attributed to Christine, while the faults can be laid clearly at my feet.

I would also like to acknowledge a number of important relationships that, while not directly tied to the production of the book, were nevertheless fundamental to the experiences needed to write it. My mother first got me interested in cholesterol and its connection to heart disease without making me paranoid about food. My first scientific mentor, Dr. Albert L. Jones, let me into his laboratory my first summer in medical school at the University of California—San Francisco, and, despite my propensity for breaking his most expensive pieces of laboratory equipment, shared his passion for lipids and research. Drs. John T. Potts, former chief of medicine at the Massachusetts General Hospital, and Henry Kronenberg, chief of the endocrine division at MGH, provided the intellectual training and financial support that enabled me to pursue a research career in the molecular biology of lipid disorders, and then enabled me to establish the Lipid Clinic and Lipid Metabolism Unit at the MGH. Christie Kuo, R.N., played a vital role in setting up the Lipid Clinic when it first opened, and then cared for every patient with extraordinary skill and compassion. Carol Whooley and Jennifer Bagan have provided the organizational skills in the Lipid Metabolism Unit that have allowed it to operate effectively while I stole the time to work on this book. Scores of medical students, residents, and clinical and research fellows have spent time in the Lipid Metabolism Unit studying the connection between cholesterol and heart disease, and providing outstanding care to the patients they encountered. And, several thousand patients with whom I have had the pleasure of working in the Lipid Clinic for nearly two decades taught me all that I know about lipid disorders.

Finally, at home, my children, James and Sarah, have helped by voicing few complaints when hospital work or writing commitments drew their father's attention away from their activities. And my wife, Dr. Sherry Haydock, who has worked with me in the clinic ever since we started it in 1986, continues to make my life, both at work and at home, a joy.

—Mason W. Freeman, M.D.

CHAPTER 1

Understanding Cholesterol: The Good, the Bad, and the Necessary

High cholesterol is a serious health problem that affects about fifty million Americans. It's a major risk factor for cardiovascular disease (CVD), which half of all men and a third of all women will get at some time in their lives. I'll spend the majority of this book on the two things my patients ask about most: how cholesterol and heart disease are connected and what they can do to optimize their cholesterol levels. But I want to take a few pages early on to clarify that cholesterol in and of itself isn't bad. While too much cholesterol can be harmful, just the right amount of it does a lot of important work in the body. But like carbohydrates in recent years, cholesterol has gotten such a bad rap that most people don't know the good it does.

Cholesterol performs three main functions:

1. It helps make the outer coating of cells.
2. It makes up the bile acids that work to digest food in the intestine.

3. It allows the body to make Vitamin D and hormones, like estrogen in women and testosterone in men.

Without cholesterol, none of these functions would take place, and without these functions, human beings wouldn't exist.

What Is Cholesterol?

Cholesterol is a fat, or lipid. It is also a sterol, from which steroid hormones are made. If you held cholesterol in your hand, you would see a waxy substance that resembles the very fine scrapings of a whitish-yellow candle. Cholesterol flows through your body via your bloodstream, but this is not a simple process. Because lipids are oil-based and blood is water-based, they don't mix. If cholesterol were simply dumped into your bloodstream, it would congeal into unusable globs. To get around this problem, the body packages cholesterol and other fats into minuscule protein-covered particles called lipoproteins (lipid + protein) that do mix easily with blood. The proteins used are known as apolipoproteins.

The fat in these particles is made up of cholesterol and triglycerides and a third material I won't discuss much, phospholipid, which helps make the whole particle stick together. Triglycerides are a particular type of fat that have three fatty acids attached to an alcohol called glycerol—hence the name. They compose about 90 percent of the fat in the food you eat. The body needs triglycerides for energy, but as with cholesterol, too much is bad for the arteries and the heart.

A Lipoprotein by Any Other Name

The two main types of lipoproteins important in a discussion on heart disease are low-density lipoproteins (LDL) and high-density lipoproteins (HDL). Though the names sound the same, these two particles are as different as night and day. The differences stem from their densities, which are a reflection of the ratio of protein to lipid; particles with more fat and less protein have a lower den-

What Are the Different Types of Fats?

Most people are vaguely familiar with the terms saturated and unsaturated fat. But what do they really mean? All fats have a similar chemical structure: a chain of carbon atoms bonded to hydrogen atoms. What differs is the length and shape of their carbon atoms and the number of hydrogen atoms. These slight structural differences create crucial differences in how the body reacts to them. I'll go into more detail about diet and cholesterol in Chapter 6, but for now, here's a primer:

- **Saturated fat.** The word *saturated* here refers to the number of hydrogen atoms these fats have. The chain of carbon atoms that makes up these fats holds as many hydrogen atoms as possible, so they're saturated. Saturated fats are unhealthy.
- **Unsaturated fat.** These have fewer hydrogen atoms and are healthy for you. There are two different kinds of unsaturated fats: polyunsaturated and monounsaturated. Polyunsaturated fats, like omega-3 fats and omega-6 fats, have four or more carbons that are not saturated with hydrogens. Monounsaturated fats have just one pair of carbon molecules that are not saturated with hydrogens.

sity than their high-protein, low-fat counterparts. There are countless other lipoproteins, some of which I'll discuss in later chapters, but in order to get a basic understanding of how cholesterol affects your body and how the food you eat affects your cholesterol levels, LDL and HDL are the ones to start with.

Low-Density Lipoproteins (LDL)

In most people, 60 to 70 percent of cholesterol is carried in LDL particles. LDL particles act as ferries, taking cholesterol to the parts of the body that need it at any given time. Unfortunately, if you have too much LDL in the bloodstream, it deposits the cholesterol into the arteries, which can cause blockages and lead to heart attacks. That's why people refer to LDL as the "bad" cholesterol. The good news is that the amount of LDL in your bloodstream is related to the amount of saturated fat and cholesterol you eat. So, most people can decrease their LDL if they follow a reduced-fat diet. When you get a fasting cholesterol test, your doctor should test for the level of LDL cholesterol.

High-Density Lipoproteins (HDL)

HDL is basically the opposite of LDL. Instead of having a lot of fat, HDL has a lot of protein. Instead of ferrying cholesterol around the body, HDL acts as a vacuum cleaner sucking up as much excess cholesterol as it can (see Figure 1.1). It picks up extra cholesterol from the cells and tissues and takes it back to the liver, which takes the cholesterol out of the particle and either uses it to make bile or recycles it. This action is thought to explain why high levels of HDL are associated with low risk for heart disease. HDL also contains antioxidant molecules that may prevent LDL from being changed into a lipoprotein that is even more likely to cause heart disease. Lifestyle changes affect HDL levels—exercise can increase them, while obesity and smoking lower them. As for diet, in general, the high-fat diets that raise LDL also raise HDL, while low-fat diets lower both. However, by carefully choosing the right foods, you can eat a diet that lowers LDL without lowering HDL, as I'll discuss in Chapter 6.

You Mean My Body Makes Cholesterol?

Cholesterol is so important to the body that it makes it itself—Mother Nature doesn't leave it up to humans to get whatever they need from diet alone. So even if you ate a completely cholesterol-free diet, your body would make the approximately 1,000 mg it needs to function properly. Your body has the ability to regulate the amount of cholesterol in the blood, producing more when your diet doesn't provide adequate amounts. The regulation of cholesterol synthesis is an elegant process that is tightly controlled.

FIGURE 1.1 HDL to the Rescue

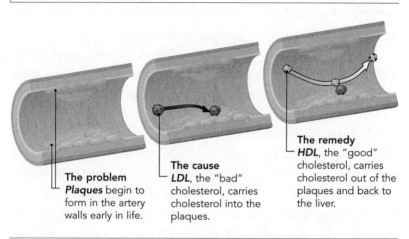

The problem
Plaques begin to
form in the artery
walls early in life.

The cause
LDL, the "bad"
cholesterol, carries
cholesterol into the
plaques.

The remedy
HDL, the "good"
cholesterol, carries
cholesterol out of the
plaques and back to
the liver.

*High cholesterol levels result in atherosclerosis, a narrowing or hardening of the
arteries that can cause heart disease, stroke, and other major health problems.
Fortunately, the body uses its own "good" cholesterol to clear out the "bad"
cholesterol before it becomes harmful.*

The system works much as your thermostat and furnace work
to regulate the temperature in your home. The thermostat in this
case is a protein that can sense the cholesterol content of a cell.
When it senses a low level of cellular cholesterol, the protein signals the genes of the cell (the furnace in this analogy) to produce
the proteins that make cholesterol. The cell makes more cholesterol, and it also makes more proteins on the cell surface that can
capture the circulating LDL particles, thereby retrieving cholesterol by bringing it in from the blood. It is this regulation that
permits the commonly used cholesterol-lowering drugs to work
so effectively, which I will describe in more detail in Chapter 8.

Almost all of the cells of the body can make the cholesterol
they need. The liver, however, is an especially efficient cholesterol
factory, efficient enough that it can afford to export much of what
it makes. The liver packages much of its cholesterol into lipoproteins that can be delivered to cells throughout the body, providing a supplement to what each cell can make on its own. This

supplement is especially important to the areas of the body that utilize a lot of cholesterol—like the testes in men and the ovaries in women, where the sex hormones are created.

In an attempt to make the public health message about keeping your cholesterol at a healthy level easy to understand, educators often don't emphasize the point that all humans make substantial quantities of cholesterol. But it's important that you understand this because it clears up confusion a lot of my patients voice. When I tell a patient that she has high cholesterol, she may say, "How could that be? I hardly eat any foods with cholesterol. My body must somehow make cholesterol—that's what's wrong!" So I have to explain that making cholesterol isn't something that she uniquely and unluckily does—all humans do it, and we wouldn't survive otherwise.

Your blood cholesterol level is determined by the sum of how much cholesterol your body makes and how much you take in from food, minus how much your body uses up or excretes. High cholesterol can result from a problem in any of the variables in that equation—your body may produce more cholesterol than it needs due to a genetic predisposition, you may be getting too much from your diet, or you may not excrete cholesterol in your bile efficiently. The fact that Americans have higher blood cholesterol levels than citizens of the Far East or Africa could be due to differences in genetic factors, but most evidence suggests that our higher cholesterol levels are largely a product of our high-fat, high-cholesterol diet.

Your body does need food to fuel the cholesterol production process, but it can be virtually any kind of food, even the cholesterol-free kind. As long as the food contains carbon—which carbohydrates, fats, and proteins all do—it provides the body with the building blocks to make its own cholesterol. Cholesterol is made out of the carbon that is recycled from the food you eat. Saturated fats, however, raise blood cholesterol levels more than other types of food, which is why people watching their cholesterol are told to avoid them. This is true even if saturated fat (which doesn't have any cholesterol in itself but is often found in foods with high cholesterol) is eaten in a cholesterol-free food. Why saturated fat does this is still something of a biological mystery.

Family History Lessons: Familial Hypercholesterolemia

There are a variety of genetic disorders that affect how the body makes lipids. In terms of heart disease risk, the most detrimental lipid disorders increase LDL levels and decrease HDL levels. The majority of these disorders are caused by a few problematic genes combined with environmental factors such as obesity or a diet high in saturated fat. As far as treatment goes, it doesn't matter if your high cholesterol is caused by problematic genes or not. Medication and lifestyle changes are still prescribed based on your HDL and LDL levels. However, the discovery of these genetic problems has greatly increased researchers' understanding of lipoproteins and cholesterol.

A family history of heart troubles can increase anyone's risk for heart disease, but for people with a gene mutation that causes extremely high cholesterol levels—and at an early age—it nearly guarantees it.

Nearly.

Kelly's father died of a heart attack at twenty-eight, before she was born. A police officer, he collapsed while trying to break up a fight. An autopsy showed that three of his coronary arteries were nearly 80 percent blocked—an unusual circumstance in such a young man. Kelly's mom is a nurse, and despite the reluctance of her doctors, she had Kelly's cholesterol tested when Kelly was one year old. The sobering result: Kelly's cholesterol was 350.

The pediatricians hadn't dealt with such a high cholesterol level in a child so young, and so they referred Kelly to a specialist. Early treatment consisted of a low-fat, low-cholesterol diet. "It wasn't nearly as bad as people might think," says Kelly. "My mom modified recipes, even for baking, and I would eat 'treats' occasionally, like pizza or cake at a birthday party. I was also very active, playing soccer, softball, taking dance classes, and swimming a lot in the summer. My mom really encouraged this, too."

While Kelly's mother had special motivation to be so vigilant, it's a good lesson for all parents. "In some ways, it was good to have to adopt a healthy lifestyle so early," she says. "It would be very hard to suddenly have to start eating a certain diet and develop the exercise habit."

In elementary school, Kelly started taking the cholesterol-lowering medication Questran, which had to be mixed into a beverage. Kelly recalls, "It tasted horrible and I usually took it during school, so it made me feel 'different' from other kids." Her mom decided against trying niacin, which is used to lower cholesterol, because of the side effects, but as a teenager Kelly did take the herbal supplement Cholestin, which helped somewhat. I first saw Kelly when she was eighteen years old, and our initial step was to try one of the statins. This step produced a dramatic improvement in her cholesterol—better results than we achieved with other drugs. I recently switched Kelly to the statin Lipitor, starting at a lower dose and working up to 80 mg/day. She took time off from her medications when pregnant and breastfeeding, but overall she has had no side effects and is looking forward to continued good results.

Kelly has familial hypocholesterolemia, specifically Frederickson type IIa. This condition is usually due to a mutation in the LDL receptor, although there are at least two other genetic mutations that could cause the same picture. Kelly's LDL is quite high, but her HDL is in a very healthy range, and she's never had a problem with high triglycerides. Her daughter, who is seven, shows no signs of cholesterol problems, but her two-year-old son's cholesterol is about 260, with a relatively low HDL level.

Kelly, like her mom, is a nurse and knows what she needs to do to protect her health and that of her children. But she is quick to point out that she leads a healthy lifestyle not only to keep her cholesterol in check. She also wants to stay healthy and live a long life for her kids and husband. And she wants to set a good example along the way. "It can be difficult sometimes. Things get hectic with a job and raising a family. Occasionally when things get crazy, I think how easy it would be to pick up dinner at a fast-food joint. And once in a while, I do, but fast food isn't part of our lifestyle."

Although she doesn't "worry" about it, Kelly knows that heart disease is still the leading cause of death for women. That knowledge almost seems inescapable based on news reports and even the ads for cholesterol-lowering drugs. Still, she says that she feels good about taking all the necessary steps to protect her heart health. "I tell my daughter that there's nothing wrong with my heart but that I have to see a specialist regularly to check up on it to keep it healthy." Her mom—and stepdad—continue to play an active role in looking after Kelly's heart health and that of her children.

The loss of Kelly's dad is tragic. Fortunately, her mom put two and two together and helped set Kelly on a healthy path that is likely to steer her away from heart problems and makes it less likely that one terrible family "tradition" will be carried forward.

The Other Source: Diet

For most people—especially those with high cholesterol—the liver and other cells aren't the body's only sources of cholesterol. Our society's typical high-fat diet also packs a powerful cholesterol punch. How can cholesterol from a hamburger and French fries eventually make its way to your heart's arteries? As you eat food with cholesterol, your intestines go through a complex process of breaking down fat molecules and building them into new molecules that the body can use (see Figure 1.2).

Intestinal enzymes rapidly dismantle the long, complex fat molecules into their component fatty acids, reassemble them into new triglyceride molecules, and package these new triglycerides—along with a small amount of cholesterol—into chylomicrons, a lipoprotein that has a very, very low density. The amount of

FIGURE 1.2 How Food Becomes Cholesterol

1 **Eating:** The food you eat contains fats, carbohydrates, and proteins. Fats and carbohydrates provide energy for all of the body's cells and, along with proteins, are necessary for the proper structure and metabolism of each cell.

2 **Digestion:** Enzymes and acids in the mouth, stomach, and intestines break fats, carbohydrates, and proteins into their smallest pieces, making it easier for them to leave the gut and enter the circulation. *In the small intestine,* free fatty acids are bundled, three at a time, to form molecules called triglycerides. The triglycerides are then bundled with cholesterol and protein to form larger particles called chylomicrons.

3 **In the circulation:** Chylomicrons, some free fatty acids, and sugars leave the cells lining the intestine and enter the circulation, traveling to every organ of the body. Free fatty acids and sugars are used by the cells of each organ for energy.

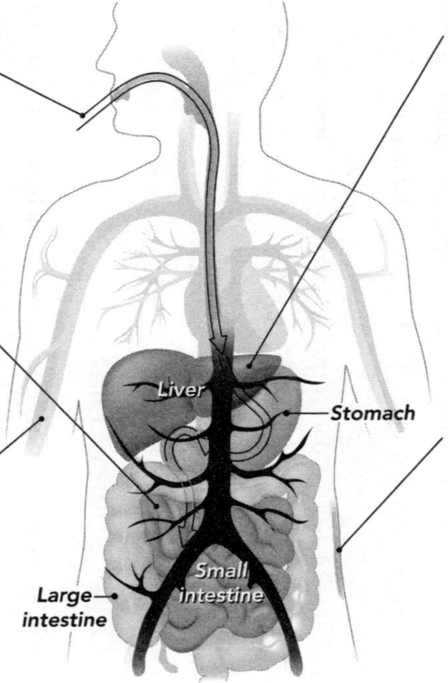

4 **The liver:** The cells of the liver play a central role in determining the different types of fats that circulate in your blood. Here, triglycerides, cholesterol, and proteins called apolipoproteins are packaged together to make larger molecules called very low-density lipoprotein. VLDL is released into the circulation, where it is transformed into low-density lipoprotein. LDL carries cholesterol to all cells of the body.

The liver also makes a molecule called high-density lipoprotein (HDL) that carries cholesterol away from the cells of the body and back to the liver.

5 **Storing energy:** Some free fatty acids are not immediately used by cells as energy but are stored away inside fat cells to provide energy in the future. Likewise, some sugars are not used immediately for energy but are instead bundled together into a molecule called glycogen, which is stored in the liver and other tissues as a future source of energy.

triglyceride-rich particles in the blood increases for several hours after a meal as the intestines release a barrage of chylomicrons filled with triglycerides.

At the same time, dietary carbohydrates and proteins that are absorbed from the intestines pass to the liver, which converts them to triglyceride molecules, packages them with apolipoproteins and cholesterol, and releases the resulting very low-density lipoproteins (VLDL) into the bloodstream. As chylomicrons and VLDL course around the body, they temporarily stick to the walls of blood vessels in muscles that need energy or in fatty tissue that stores energy. Enzymes come along and remove most of their load of triglyceride molecules, which are then transported inside the muscle or fat cells. As triglyceride is drained from the chylomicron or VLDL particles, their protective protein coats are rearranged and reconfigured, essentially giving them a new address label that can be read by the liver or other tissues that take up lipoproteins.

Both chylomicrons and VLDL become more and more dense as they give up their low-density fatty cargo. Eventually, all that remains is the packaging material—the protein and cholesterol—and a fraction of the original triglyceride. Chylomicron remnants don't linger in the circulation—the liver filters them from the system and recycles their components.

Many of the triglyceride-depleted VLDL remnants, though, keep circulating and undergo further modification of their lipid and protein content. Eventually these particles are converted to LDL. Virtually all cells in the body can take up and use LDL for their individual needs. But because there are usually more LDL particles in circulation at any one time than your body can use, it's your liver's job to clear the excess from the blood and use it to make more bile acids or new lipoproteins. If the liver can't keep up with the supply of LDL, these particles can come to rest in the wrong places, typically in the lining of blood vessels. In extreme cases, they may settle in the skin and tendons, where they form yellow deposits.

HDL is made by the liver and intestines and has two main jobs. HDL particles give chylomicrons and VLDL the proteins that signal the liver to trap them and extract their fat. They also sponge up excess cholesterol from the linings of blood vessels and elsewhere and carry it off to the liver for disposal.

People who can't package lipoproteins effectively in the liver because of a genetic mutation still carry out the majority of the body's functions quite well, although they do tend to have problems absorbing vitamins A, D, E, and K and often have blood cell and neurological problems as a result. Those vitamins are fat-soluble, meaning they are carried in the fat particles that make up lipoproteins, so if the body can't package these molecules, it can't absorb the vitamins.

Why You Need to Know

When patients come to me because they have high cholesterol, I'm always amazed at how interested they are not only in the "how-they-can-get-better" part but also in why they have a problem. I think the knowledge of the two goes hand in hand. Knowing how cholesterol is made in the body and how cholesterol is absorbed from food is the foundation for understanding how the right eating plan and, when necessary, cholesterol-lowering drugs, are effective.

CHAPTER 2

Heart Disease Primer

Cholesterol seems to have taken on a life of its own in today's society. People brag about their levels or bemoan them, but often without any real understanding of the role cholesterol plays in causing heart disease. Some of my patients expend enormous emotional energy worrying about their cholesterol levels, while ignoring other issues that play an equally important role in causing the coronary arteries to be blocked. In most people, cholesterol is only one factor—though a very important one—in the complex process that leads to atherosclerotic heart disease. And atherosclerotic heart disease has been the number one killer of Americans every year since 1921. Lowering your blood cholesterol is one of the five basic health-care steps that will keep you from becoming a heart disease statistic, along with not smoking, eating right, exercising, and controlling your blood pressure.

What Is Heart Disease?

Your heart muscle (myocardium) is about the size of your clenched fist. It sits behind the breastbone and beats constantly, starting shortly after conception and continuing for more than seventy years in most Americans. Although it was once thought to be the seat of the soul, the heart is really a remarkable pump: it pumps oxygenated blood to all the cells in the human body,

FIGURE 2.1 Anatomy of a Heart

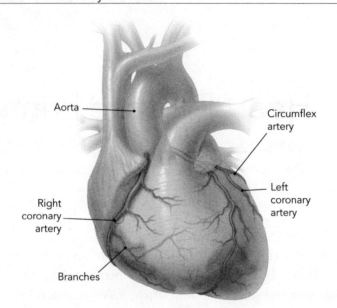

including its own cells, bringing them needed nourishment and hormones, and it sends the used or deoxygenated blood back to the lungs so the cycle can begin again. The major artery that delivers blood from the heart to the rest of the body is called the aorta. The aorta has two branch arteries, the right and left coronary arteries, which bring blood to the heart. These two arteries each branch into progressively smaller and smaller channels. The left coronary artery typically splits into two large branches that are responsible for supplying nutrients to the cardiac muscle that drives blood throughout the body (see Figure 2.1).

Coronary artery disease (CAD) begins with a buildup of plaque in either the left or right coronary artery or their branches. This reduces the blood flow to the heart, but early on, this reduction is not severe enough to compromise heart muscle function or to produce any symptoms. Later, as the plaque enlarges and further reduces blood flow, blood flow interruption can reach the critical point where the heart muscle no longer gets adequate oxygen delivery when it is working vigorously (as when you exercise).

Ischemia is the medical word for this interruption. A temporary or partial interruption in the supply of blood, known as mild ischemia, will injure the myocardium and cause the chest pain known as angina. A prolonged or complete interruption, known as severe ischemia, will kill myocardial cells and cause a heart attack. You can think of a coronary blockage as a car accident that blocks the flow of traffic through one of a handful of roads that serve a very important city. The more neighborhoods served by a road, the more disruptive a blockage is to the life of the city. Generally, the more heart muscle a coronary artery feeds, the more devastating its failure is to the heart.

There are exceptions to this rule. For example, a relatively minor blockage can set off extreme electrical instability in the heart that can prove fatal because the heart muscle can no longer contract in a coordinated fashion. If the function of the electrical circuits could be restored in a timely fashion, through the use of drugs or a defibrillator, this injury might not even result in a detectable loss in muscle-pumping power.

Heart-shocking devices called defibrillators were once available only in hospitals and ambulances, but they're now popping up in public places. You can find these public versions, called automated external defibrillators, in airports, movie theaters, fitness centers, casinos, malls, office buildings, and elsewhere. They are so easy to use that sixth graders who have never seen one before can master them in a minute or so. The machines have easy-to-understand instructions on them, and it's basically just a matter of turning on the machine, attaching the pads to the victim's bare chest—one on the upper part of the person's right chest and the other on the left side near the armpit—waiting for the machine to analyze the heart rhythm, and pressing the shock or rescue button if the machine tells you to do so. Using these machines could save a life, as can performing cardiac resuscitation methods like CPR.

How Is Cardiac Arrest Different from a Heart Attack?

Most people think of a heart attack as something that happens quickly and causes someone to grab his or her chest and fall to the ground. That's actually a picture of cardiac arrest. A heart attack, as the term is commonly used today, generally means the blockage of an artery in the heart that kills some heart muscle. (Medically speaking, this is a myocardial infarction.) A heart attack usually gives some warning. Chest pain or other symptoms can prompt someone to get help before the blockage totally disrupts the heart's rhythm.

Cardiac arrest, though, strikes suddenly and out of the blue. Most cardiac arrests occur when the heart's powerful lower chambers, the ventricles, start beating very fast (ventricular tachycardia [ta-kih-CAR-dee-uh]) or fast and chaotically (ventricular fibrillation). Either one of these makes it impossible for the heart to pump blood to the body.

After just five seconds without blood circulation, a person passes out. In another few seconds, the lack of oxygen in the brain causes nerves to start firing, making the muscles twitch and the eyes roll back. Even that activity stops in less than a minute. The chances of surviving a cardiac arrest fall about 10 percent for each minute the heart stays in ventricular fibrillation. Shock the heart back into a normal rhythm within two minutes, and the victim has an 80 percent chance of surviving. Deliver that shock after seven minutes—the average time it takes an emergency medical team to arrive in many cities—and the odds are less than 30 percent.

If someone near you goes into cardiac arrest, calling 911 is a must. CPR is also important because it keeps blood flowing to the brain and other vital organs. If there's an automated external defibrillator nearby, use it following the instructions on the device.

How Heart Disease Happens

What causes the blockages that set off these events? In a word, atherosclerosis. The term is a combination of two Greek words: *athere*, meaning pudding, and *sclerosis*, meaning hardening. The root words describe what happens in atherosclerosis: the artery walls become filled with soft, mushy deposits that eventually harden to make the artery stiff and narrow. Put simply, the arteries get clogged in the same way the pipe in your bathroom sink might when too much debris sticks to its walls, blocking the flow of water. Though the pipe analogy might make artery clogging seem straightforward, it's a fairly complicated process. There are four steps that occur in what is known as the coronary cascade to a heart attack (see Figure 2.2).

Step 1: Weakened Lining

The first step in the road to heart disease appears to require an elevated level of blood cholesterol, carried in one of the lipoprotein particles, particularly LDL. When there's excess LDL in the bloodstream, some of it moves out of the blood and into the artery wall. The higher the LDL level, the more LDL finds its way into the artery wall.

Every artery wall has three layers (see Figure 2.3). The inner layer, or *intima*, has a delicate, single layer of cells (called *endothelial cells*) between it and the bloodstream, which acts like a kind of Teflon coating for the artery, making it possible for the blood to flow smoothly through the vessel. These cells also send out signals to recruit inflammatory cells and help those cells stick in the right locations so they can penetrate into the tissues when they are needed to help clear away debris or infectious agents.

High cholesterol, high blood pressure, smoking, and diabetes, among other things, can disrupt the function of endothelial cells. This disruption can take on many forms—it may increase or

FIGURE 2.2 How Heart Disease Happens

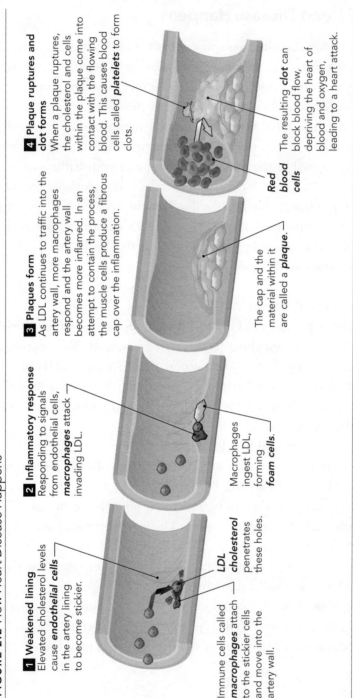

1 Weakened lining
Elevated cholesterol levels cause *endothelial cells* in the artery lining to become stickier.

Immune cells called *macrophages* attach to the stickier cells and move into the artery wall.

LDL cholesterol penetrates these holes.

2 Inflammatory response
Responding to signals from endothelial cells, *macrophages* attack invading LDL.

Macrophages ingest LDL, forming *foam cells*.

3 Plaques form
As LDL continues to traffic into the artery wall, more macrophages respond and the artery wall becomes more inflamed. In an attempt to contain the process, the muscle cells produce a fibrous cap over the inflammation.

The cap and the material within it are called a *plaque*.

4 Plaque ruptures and clot forms
When a plaque ruptures, the cholesterol and cells within the plaque come into contact with the flowing blood. This causes blood cells called *platelets* to form clots.

Red blood cells

The resulting *clot* can block blood flow, depriving the heart of blood and oxygen, leading to a heart attack.

FIGURE 2.3 Anatomy of an Artery

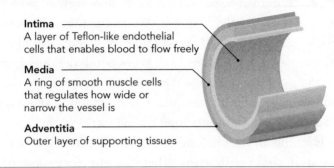

Intima
A layer of Teflon-like endothelial
cells that enables blood to flow freely

Media
A ring of smooth muscle cells
that regulates how wide or
narrow the vessel is

Adventitia
Outer layer of supporting tissues

decrease levels of the constricting and relaxing hormones as well as the signals that recruit inflammatory cells. The regulation of blood flow and blood pressure can be disrupted. The endothelial cells can also loosen their attachment to the intimal layer and to each other, resulting in gaps in the lining.

No matter what a person's cholesterol level is, the endothelial cells ship some LDL from the blood into the intimal layer. However, the higher the LDL concentration in the blood, the more the endothelial cells ship LDL into the artery wall. The LDL may also take advantage of some of the breaches in the lining layer and directly penetrate to the interior of the artery wall.

Step 2: Inflammatory Response

These events generate an inflammatory response. The endothelial cells at key locations in the arteries release chemical messengers called chemokines, which in turn call immune cells known as macrophages to the scene. Macrophages ingest the LDL and become engorged with cholesterol, forming a foam cell (so named because the cholesterol makes the cells look foamy). Though the macrophages are trying to clear away the LDL and clean up any debris left in the artery wall, they end up making things worse because they continue to call for reinforcements in the war against the LDL, and the extra cells cause more clogging of the arteries.

We think this occurs because macrophages are designed to fight off infectious microbes, that is, to kill their prey, control the infection, and then quietly disappear. When the prey is instead a lipid particle that is continually produced by the body, it is like an infection that never ends. More LDL keeps being deposited, and more macrophages keep getting called to clean up the mess. These steps result in a chronic and sustained inflammation in the artery wall. Ultimately, the accumulation of cholesterol in the macrophage kills it, and all the cholesterol in the cell gets released into the artery wall, along with many other inflammatory substances contained in macrophages, further inflaming the process.

Step 3: Plaques Form

In an attempt to wall off this inflammation, the body signals the smooth muscle cells to proliferate and to make more fibrous material to contain the process. Eventually, a cap forms over the inflammation. This is the birth of a plaque that can narrow the artery. Plaques vary in size, and there is evidence that some early stages of plaque formation are reversible, whereas later stages are permanent. Most of us probably form and resolve small plaques throughout much of our lives. Studies in teenagers who have died from traumatic events, such as car accidents, have shown early-stage plaques in the arteries of even these very young men and women.

Step 4: Clot Causes Heart Attack

Though the reduced blood flow caused by the plaque and inflammation taxes the heart, it doesn't usually cause a heart attack. Heart attacks occur when the plaque ruptures. Plaque deposits teem with inflammatory cells (particularly macrophages and other inflammatory cells called T-lymphocytes) as well as cholesterol. The more inflammatory cells and cholesterol—and the thinner the cap that covers them—the more unstable the plaque. This sets the stage for disaster. T-cells slow the production of the fibrous materials that strengthen the cap (such as collagen), and macrophages produce enzymes that degrade collagen. This two-pronged attack degrades the cap until it breaks.

Large plaques, of course, narrow the arteries more than small plaques (think of a truck blocking a tunnel as opposed to a car), but that doesn't necessarily mean they are more dangerous. In fact, research suggests the reverse. About two-thirds of all heart attacks result from the rupture of smaller plaques—those that narrow coronary arteries only by 40 percent to 60 percent. Though large plaques narrow the arteries by 70 percent to 80 percent, they tend to be covered by thicker caps with fewer inflammatory cells underneath. This suggests a successful walling off of the inflammatory process. Smaller plaques tend to have thinner caps that are usually associated with the presence of more inflammatory cells. These two factors make the smaller caps more susceptible to rupture.

Once the cap breaks, blood seeps into the inner layer of the artery wall rather than flowing smoothly over the endothelial cell lining. This contact triggers the release of clotting factors, just as a cut to your finger would. Small clotting particles called platelets are activated at such wound sites and play a key role in the clotting and wound-healing process. The problem is that in the case of an atherosclerotic plaque rupture, the wound is inside the artery wall. Having a big scab covering a skin wound may be unsightly, but it isn't life threatening. In the coronary arteries, however, the clot further blocks the blood flow. Going back to the tunnel metaphor, the clot serves as an additional car that stalls in the one lane of traffic that had been moving around the accident. This clot is known as a thrombus. Deprived of blood and oxygen, the portion of the heart muscle that depends on this artery begins to die. This process is known medically as a myocardial infarction or MI (em-eye). In everyday language, it's a heart attack.

What a Heart Attack Feels Like

I hope you'll get diagnosed and treated long before heart disease leads to a heart attack, but you should know the warning signs just in case. Unlike in the movies, where a person having a heart attack gropes his chest (and in the movies, unlike reality, it's

An LDL Controversy

Although LDL is thought to be the major cholesterol-carrying culprit causing heart disease, there is still scientific controversy over the form LDL must take to cause atherosclerosis. For nearly twenty years, atherosclerosis researchers have hypothesized that LDL must change once it's in the artery wall in order to cause artery blockages. The dominant view has been that LDL must first be oxidized to a more inflammatory form in order to cause serious artery wall damage. Oxidation is the chemical reaction that causes metals to rust by changing the structure of the metals' molecules. Similarly, oxidation may change the chemical structure of LDL molecules by breaking down large fat-containing molecular chains. Although there are literally thousands of studies that have suggested a role for oxidized LDL in causing heart disease, the use of antioxidants, such as vitamin E, has not resulted in any convincing decline in atherosclerosis in humans. This isn't proof that oxidation is unimportant, it's just that we don't know yet. The precise form LDL must take to set off atherosclerotic plaque formation remains a bit of a mystery, but the link between high LDL levels and coronary disease is firmly established.

almost always a man) and falls to the floor, the symptoms of a real-life heart attack are often more subtle. They differ between men and women and from person to person. Generally, men will report the following:

- Pain or discomfort in the chest that radiates to the shoulder or arms, to the upper back near the shoulder blades, or to the neck or jaw
- Uncomfortable pressure, tightness, fullness, or ache at the center of the chest
- Shortness of breath, sweating, nausea, or dizziness

Women, on the other hand, usually report the following:

A Word About Heart Attack Risk

The process that leads to an MI is complex. Not only does the LDL have to get into the artery wall, but all of the subsequent steps described must also occur for a plaque to rupture and cause a heart attack. In addition to a person's cholesterol level, genetic and environmental variables influence all of the steps in the process. This is why a doctor can't predict with certainty whether a person will have a heart attack simply based on an LDL cholesterol level. Children and young adults with rare genetic abnormalities that produce LDL levels that are five to ten times higher than normal are the exception to that statement. Without appropriate therapy, heart disease is a certainty for them. The rest of us have to rely primarily on statistical predictions based on our current understanding of all of the risk factors that predispose to heart disease. (You can calculate your risk using the Heart Attack Calculator in Chapter 5.)

- Pain in both arms or shoulders
- Chest cramping or dull pain between the breasts
- Shortness of breath
- Feeling of indigestion
- Lower abdominal pain
- Severe fatigue (the least specific symptom, usually not caused by a heart attack)

What to Do if You're Having a Heart Attack

If you or someone around you experiences the heart attack warning signs previously listed, follow these three simple steps:

1. **Call 911.** You may be reluctant to call for help, especially if you're not sure whether your discomfort is caused by a heart attack or indigestion, but doing so will get you better—and safer—treatment. Calling for an ambulance is like bringing

an emergency room to you. Emergency medical personnel can restart your heart if it stops beating. They can give you oxygen to help you breathe and aspirin and other treatments to prevent further blood clots.

Another good reason for emergency transport is quicker treatment once you get to the hospital. Heart attack victims who arrive by ambulance receive appropriate treatment sooner than those who arrive by car. If, for some reason, you have a family member or friend drive you to the hospital, tell the person at the desk, "I think I'm having a heart attack" in no uncertain terms. Don't be wishy-washy about it. Sitting in the waiting room because you told the desk clerk that it wasn't an emergency won't do you any good. Whatever you do, don't drive yourself to the hospital.

2. **Chew a regular-strength aspirin.** Aspirin "poisons" platelets so that they do not form clots well. Some people who use aspirin occasionally may notice that they bleed longer from small cuts or may bruise more easily if they have taken aspirin recently. This minor annoyance can be a lifesaver, however, when platelets threaten to clump inside the coronary artery and block blood flow to the heart. If you can't chew an aspirin, mash it up in a glass of water and drink it down. It's important not to take an aspirin whole; it can take too long for the body to break it down and absorb it.

3. **Call a friend or family member.** If you're alone, immediately call someone and tell him or her what's going on.

Time Is Not on Your Side if You're Having a Heart Attack

The average person waits two hours or more after the onset of heart attack symptoms to call for help, and one in four people waits more than five hours. It's not ignorance—it takes the average doctor who is having a heart attack two hours, too. Most people wait because they aren't sure if they're really having a heart attack and can't decide whether to seek medical care.

It's easy to write off heart attack symptoms as something else. Chest pain can arise from stress- or activity-related angina. That hot, heavy feeling in the chest could be heartburn or gas. An ache in the left arm or jaw could be arthritis or the aftermath of snow shoveling.

Unfortunately, there's no simple rule of thumb that separates a heart attack from a false alarm. And you'll probably have a hard time being objective about it, which is why it's so important to let a professional make an informed and unbiased judgment.

Another deterrent is more personal. People don't want to look foolish if it's a false alarm or don't want to worry or bother others. Keep in mind what I tell my patients (and my family!): it's much easier to live with embarrassment than with a damaged heart. So, if you feel like you're having a heart attack and the symptoms last more than a few minutes, call 911 (or your local emergency number) sooner rather than later.

A Heart Attack Plan

Of course you don't want to think that you'll have a heart attack. But with about a million Americans having one each year, it's better to be safe than sorry. Here are some additional steps you can take to make sure you get the best care possible if you have a heart attack:

- Make packages that include a list of medications you're taking and those you are allergic to, as well as the name(s) of an emergency contact. Keep a package near the phone at home and work and another in your car. If you know you have heart disease, also include instructions or a letter from your doctor and a copy of your latest electrocardiogram (EKG).
- Check your house or apartment building to make sure it has a number that's clearly visible from the street.

- Think through what you would do if you had heart attack symptoms at home, at work, or somewhere else.
- Decide who would take care of children, an ailing spouse or parent, or anyone else you usually care for. In a pinch, emergency medical personnel will try to reach a friend or relative (or the police, if necessary) to arrange emergency care for your dependents.
- Go over with your family and friends the warning signs of a heart attack and the importance of quickly calling 911 if those signs last for more than a few minutes.

CHAPTER 3

If You Know You Have Heart Disease

Once you've received a diagnosis of coronary artery disease—whether or not you've had a heart attack—you face the question of what's the best way to treat it. This question is complex, and the answer continues to evolve as new therapies become available and new studies clarify which patients benefit most from which treatments. However, one basic principle holds true: you'll need a close, continuing relationship with your primary care physician and a cardiologist.

The goals of treatment are to keep your condition stable, prevent further damage to your heart, and, ideally, reverse some of the atherosclerosis in your coronary arteries. It's not surprising that measures for preventing heart disease are also effective in controlling it. Keep that in mind when you're reading about the risk factors you can change on pages 50–66. You'll also want to look over Chapters 6 and 7, which discuss lifestyle changes to improve cholesterol and lower your chance of heart disease.

All patients with coronary artery disease need to exercise and to discuss the progress of their exercise program regularly and in detail with their physicians. Aerobic exercise, such as walking, bicycling, or swimming, can help you lose weight or maintain a normal weight and increase the amount of work you can do with less strain on your heart. You'll also need to follow a heart-healthy diet, use strategies to control stress, and—it almost goes without saying—not smoke.

Medications

Along with healthy eating and regular exercise, medications are the first-line treatment for controlling coronary artery disease. Some drugs help prevent angina or eliminate chest pain during angina episodes. Others lower blood pressure or help prevent blood clots. Most people with heart disease need to take more than one medication. The specific combination of drugs will depend on your particular symptoms and risk factors.

Beta-Blockers

Beta-blockers are among the most commonly used drugs for controlling interruptions in blood flow to the heart and high blood pressure, and for good reason—these drugs have been shown to improve survival rates after heart attacks, and they are especially effective at minimizing chest pain brought on by exercise.

There are many types of beta-blockers on the market, but all act by interfering with adrenaline, a hormone that normally stimulates the heart to beat faster and stronger. Beta-blockers slow the heart rate and decrease cardiac output, lowering blood pressure and decreasing the amount of work the heart must do. By lowering the oxygen needs of the heart, beta-blockers help prevent or relieve ischemia.

People with asthma, heart failure, or diabetes should be cautious when taking beta-blockers because they could worsen these conditions. However, some of the newer beta-blockers are less likely to cause side effects because they act more selectively on the heart than on other parts of the body. Despite these problems, beta-blockers are so effective in treating coronary artery disease that doctors often try them in patients with problems such as heart failure or diabetes because the benefits outweigh the risks.

Nitroglycerin

Nitroglycerin and other nitrate compounds help prevent or stop ischemia in several ways. They relax the muscles in the walls of the blood vessels, causing arteries and veins to dilate. When the coronary arteries dilate in response to nitroglycerin, the heart's blood supply increases. Nitrates also reduce the heart's work by lowering the body's blood pressure and the pressure within the heart's chambers. As a result, the heart requires less oxygen and places fewer demands on the coronary arteries. Nitroglycerin comes in many forms: pills, an aerosol, a skin patch, and an ointment that can be applied to the skin.

Angiotensin Converting Enzyme (ACE) Inhibitors

ACE inhibitors are a class of blood pressure drugs that works by dilating blood vessels. In addition to controlling high blood pressure, ACE inhibitors have long been prescribed for people with heart failure. Recent studies have shown that these drugs also help people with coronary artery disease and those at high risk for developing it.

The HOPE (Heart Outcomes Prevention Evaluation) trial, an ongoing study of heart disease prevention, has found that ACE inhibitors not only dilate blood vessels but also help slow the progression of atherosclerosis.

Calcium Channel Blockers

Like beta-blockers, calcium channel blockers control high blood pressure. Calcium channel blockers are vasodilators, meaning they dilate the coronary arteries. By doing so, they increase blood flow to the heart and cut its workload by reducing blood pressure and the force of the heart's contractions.

In contrast to beta-blockers, there is thus far no evidence that calcium channel blockers improve survival after a heart attack in patients with coronary artery disease. But they are useful for patients who don't get adequate relief from beta-blockers or nitrates. And calcium channel blockers are more effective than beta-blockers for preventing angina due to episodes of coronary artery constriction, often called coronary spasm.

Aspirin

One of the pleasant surprises of the past two decades is the benefit of aspirin for patients with coronary artery disease. This common, inexpensive drug helps protect survivors of heart attack and stroke from subsequent heart attacks and death, and it even helps reduce the number of deaths that occur within the first hours following a heart attack.

Aspirin appears to work by preventing platelets from clumping together, which can block the blood flow to the heart. Randomized trials have provided clear evidence of aspirin's value in both preventing and treating cardiovascular diseases. Early studies focused on patients who'd already suffered a heart attack or stroke, or on people with unstable forms of angina or a history of transient ischemic attacks (TIAs)—brief and reversible stroke-like episodes. For such patients, regular aspirin use significantly decreased the risk for fatal and nonfatal strokes or heart attacks. A standard dose of aspirin to prevent heart attack is 81 mg per day.

Despite aspirin's benefits, it also has some drawbacks. It can increase the risk for the less common form of stroke caused by bleeding into the brain, and it also makes significant gastrointestinal bleeding more likely. What does that mean for you? The U.S. Preventive Services Task Force, an independent panel of experts that reviews the evidence for prevention strategies and makes recommendations based on that evidence, supports the use of aspirin for people who already have heart disease or don't yet have it but are at relatively high risk. When balancing the risk of heart disease versus aspirin's risks, the tipping point seems to be about 6 percent: for people with a ten-year heart disease risk of 6 percent or higher, the benefits of taking aspiring outweigh the harm. For people with a risk below 6 percent, they don't. Using the 6 percent rule, an aspirin a day probably makes sense for the following people:

- Anyone who has had a heart attack
- Anyone diagnosed with coronary artery disease, peripheral artery disease, or a stroke or ministroke due to a blocked artery
- Adults with diabetes, because this condition often leads to heart disease
- Adults with the "metabolic syndrome," a combination of obesity, high blood pressure, and high levels of cholesterol and blood sugar
- Healthy people with a 6 percent or greater chance of having a heart attack over the next ten years, including many men over age forty and women who have passed menopause

Although this list makes it look as if everyone should be taking aspirin, that's certainly not the case. It isn't a good option if you are prone to gastrointestinal bleeding or have had a hemorrhagic stroke, even if your heart attack risk is above 6 percent.

Plavix

Plavix (clopidogrel bisulfate) is a drug that inhibits the action of platelets, much as aspirin does. It has been shown to reduce the risk of cardiovascular events only in people who've already had a heart attack or stroke, or who have the artery narrowing known as peripheral vascular disease. The Food and Drug Administration (FDA) has approved Plavix for use in people with a recent heart attack or stroke, established vascular disease, or a newly placed stent to open up a closed coronary artery. Plavix has some serious side effects, particularly excessive bleeding. This is especially dangerous if the bleeding occurs in the brain, where it could result in a hemorrhagic stroke. The drug also causes skin rashes and diarrhea in some users.

In at least one study of patients with a recent heart attack, stroke, or vascular disease, Plavix was slightly better than aspirin at preventing a subsequent serious cardiovascular event. It also caused less stomach upset and bleeding in the stomach than aspirin. But Plavix is much more expensive than aspirin and hasn't been tested as widely or as well.

Hormone Replacement Therapy (HRT)

Until recently, doctors often prescribed hormone replacement therapy to postmenopausal women, not only to help control the symptoms of menopause, but also to reduce their risk for coronary artery disease. They had reason for doing so—numerous large observational studies concluded that those taking estrogen after menopause were one-third to one-half as likely to have heart attacks or develop cardiovascular disease as those who didn't.

But more recent randomized controlled trials burst the HRT bubble. Several large trials have concluded that hormone replacement therapy doesn't help prevent heart problems and may even cause them.

The American Heart Association now advises physicians not to prescribe hormone replacement therapy solely to prevent heart attacks and strokes in women with cardiovascular disease. But some experts believe that future research may still determine that, for some women, hormone replacement therapy helps prevent heart disease. Most of the clinical trials thus far have focused on women well beyond menopause—the average age has been sixty-seven. But hormone replacement therapy might be beneficial when started by younger women who have just gone through menopause.

Until more and better information is available, women should discuss hormone replacement therapy with their doctor. The decision is personal and should be based on a woman's postmenopausal symptoms as well as her risks for breast cancer, endometrial cancer, heart disease, osteoporosis, and other hormone-related conditions. Here are the recommendations that I generally give to my patients:

- If you have heart disease, don't start hormone replacement therapy just to treat this condition or to prevent a heart attack. Instead, focus on proven prevention strategies such as eating healthily, getting more exercise, controlling blood pressure, and lowering cholesterol. Estrogen that was prescribed to treat high cholesterol should be replaced with a cholesterol-lowering medication, such as one of the statin drugs discussed in Chapter 8.

- If you've been on hormone replacement therapy for several years, you should discuss with your doctor whether you still need this treatment, but you're probably past the early period of increased risk. The American Heart Association recommends that women stop hormone replacement therapy at least temporarily following a heart attack or if they are confined to bed for some reason, and that they start again only for reasons other than heart health. Also, women who take hormone replacement therapy face a small increased risk for breast cancer. So it's a good idea to work with your doctor to evaluate your risk for breast cancer.

- If you don't have heart disease, base your decision about whether to use hormone replacement therapy on its proven ability to relieve menopausal symptoms. But keep in mind that there are a variety of alternatives to taking an estrogen pill for these problems.

Selective Estrogen Receptor Modulators

These new drugs, sometimes called "designer estrogens," appear to affect blood lipids in much the same way that estrogen does but possibly without the increased risk for breast cancer and endometrial cancer associated with hormone replacement therapy. Raloxifene (Evista), one of these drugs, has been shown to decrease levels of LDL, but unlike estrogen does not reliably elevate HDL cholesterol, though it may increase one of the HDL subfractions. Also unlike estrogen, raloxifene doesn't elevate triglyceride levels. Raloxifene is approved for osteoporosis prevention, and recent preliminary studies suggest that it may be effective at reducing breast cancer risk. Like estrogen, however, it does increase the risk of blood clots in the legs. Overall, I don't use raloxifene as a primary treatment for lipid problems, but if a woman needs a drug to treat her osteoporosis, raloxifene's generally favorable effects on lipids make it a reasonable choice. If further trials show that this drug does help prevent breast cancer, its use may become much more widespread.

Cholesterol-Lowering Drugs

Of course, cholesterol-lowering drugs can significantly help lower your risk of heart disease. I'll go into greater detail on them in Chapter 8.

Procedures to Open Blocked Arteries

With the help of medications, most patients with coronary artery disease can live normal lives that have few limitations. However, some patients benefit from procedures that restore blood flow to areas of the heart muscle that have been affected by a blocked artery.

The two main procedures are angioplasty—which is performed by cardiologists—and coronary artery bypass graft surgery (CABG)—which is performed by heart surgeons. These procedures can relieve angina and improve life expectancy, but they also carry a small risk for heart attack, stroke, and other complications, including death. Therefore, they are generally reserved for patients whose symptoms can't be adequately controlled with medications and those who are at very high risk for a heart attack.

Before Angioplasty or Surgery: Cardiac Catheterization

Before you get either an angioplasty or cardiac surgery, your doctor will have to perform a cardiac catheterization. During this procedure, pictures are taken of blockages in the arteries of your heart. To do this, the doctor will insert a catheter (a thin, hollow plastic tube) into a large artery—usually in your groin, but possibly in an arm or wrist—after you receive local anesthetics. The doctor then moves the catheter along the artery until it reaches your aorta. The tip of the catheter is pushed up the aorta until it reaches the heart. Then it is gently pushed into the coronary arteries that supply blood directly to your heart muscle. At this point, a contrast dye will be injected through the catheter to help the blood vessels show up better on the x-ray, illuminating whether the artery is blocked or narrowed. If the cardiologist performing the catheterization thinks the artery is blocked enough to call for an angioplasty, it can be done immediately. If cardiac surgery is required, the heart surgeon will use pictures obtained during the catheterization as a guide.

Angioplasty

As already described, angioplasty starts with the physician inserting a catheter into an artery and guiding it through the blood vessels to the openings of the coronary arteries. Inside this catheter is an even thinner catheter that has an inflatable balloon near its tip. And inside that catheter is a wire with a soft tip that can snake through tight narrowings and punch through clots but is unlikely to damage the wall of the coronary artery (see Figure 3.1).

The cardiologist guides the wire gently down the artery until the tip is beyond the narrowing. (When the coronary artery is completely blocked, the physician may try to push the wire through the obstruction.) Once the wire has crossed the blockage, the catheter with the balloon slides down the wire until the balloon is adjacent to the atherosclerotic plaque.

From outside the body, the physician inflates the balloon, which cracks and compresses the atherosclerotic plaque, stretches the underlying normal arterial wall, and so widens the artery.

When the procedure works well, the vessel remains wide open, and the patient's angina symptoms are alleviated. However, a relatively common problem is restenosis, a renarrowing of the artery at the same spot. Restenosis usually happens within three to six months of the original procedure. It is not surprising that it could occur, because an angioplasty is a temporary measure: the balloon expands to squash the plaque and widen the center of the artery, and then the balloon is deflated and pulled out of the body. Nothing is left in place to keep the artery open.

FIGURE 3.1 Balloon Angioplasty

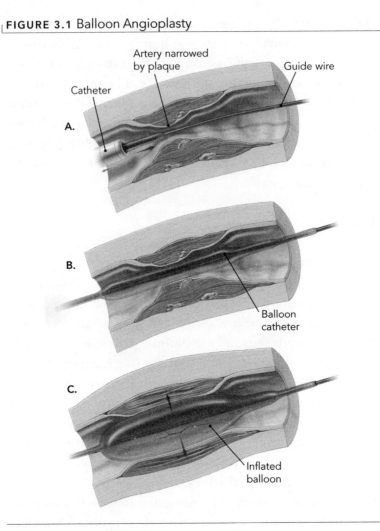

To open an artery narrowed by plaque, the cardiologist feeds a catheter to the site of the blockage and threads a thin, flexible guide wire through the narrowing (A). The balloon catheter advances along the guide wire until it's positioned directly inside the narrowed area (B). As the balloon inflates, the plaque stretches and cracks, allowing freer passage of blood through the now reopened artery (C).

About a decade ago, 25 percent to 35 percent of patients who underwent angioplasty developed restenosis that was so significant that they needed a second procedure. To reduce the chance of restenosis, cardiologists began using a device called a stent. A stent is small tube made of an expandable metal mesh that is inserted at the area of narrowing and left in place. The use of stents has lowered the restenosis rate to 10 percent to 20 percent, and newer types of stents appear even more effective. Today, more than 70 percent of people who undergo angioplasty have stents inserted.

To place the stent, the doctor uses the same balloon catheter used in angioplasty. The collapsed stent is wrapped over a balloon catheter. When the balloon is inflated at the site of the blockage, the stent also expands and remains expanded even when the balloon inside it has been deflated. The doctor pulls the balloon-tipped catheter out of the body and leaves the expanded stent in place.

Even after this procedure, a blood vessel can close up again. This usually occurs because of a process called intimal hyperplasia. The atherosclerotic plaque, stimulated by immune system cells in the lining of the artery, starts to grow through the small holes in the wire mesh of the stent. However, new stents coated with drugs help prevent that from happening (see Figure 3.2). The coating prevents restenosis by stopping the cells lining the vessel wall from vigorously reproducing.

Drug-coated stents have been widely available for only a couple of years, but they have already made a huge impact on our treatment of patients with coronary artery disease. Nowadays, almost everyone who has a stent procedure gets one coated with an immunosuppressant drug. As this book goes to press, two different types of coated stents have been approved for use. There have been some manufacturing problems with each of them that can cause rare but serious complications as the stent is being placed in the artery. The companies that make these stents are working to fix the problem, and there is no reported risk to people who have previously received one of these stents: the rare complications occur only as the stents are being placed in a person's body. We expect that by the time this book is published, the manufacturing problems will have been fixed and this risk eliminated.

Following a stent procedure, patients take aspirin—and sometimes other drugs that thin the blood—in order to prevent clotting and, therefore, restenosis. Aspirin must be taken indefinitely,

FIGURE 3.2 Drug-Coated Stents

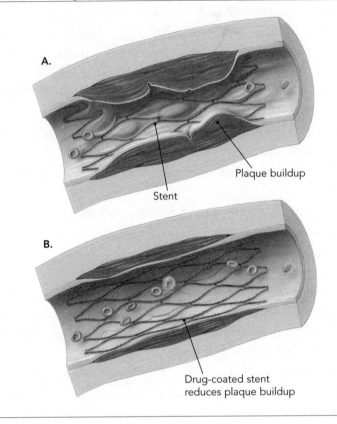

One way to prop open a blood vessel is to insert a mesh cage called a stent into the artery. But clots can form and cause the artery to renarrow (A). To help keep such arteries clear, scientists have developed drug-coated stents (B).

and some patients take another blood thinner for two to four weeks following surgery. Two commonly used blood thinners are ticlopidine and clopidogrel. Patients need to take these drugs regardless of whether they receive drug-coated stents or the regular, uncoated variety.

About one person in five is born with a tendency to resist the blood-thinning effects of aspirin. Some doctors are now starting to test for such aspirin resistance and are emphasizing the use of other blood-thinning drugs when tests show that a person is aspirin resistant. Other doctors do not believe that the current

Fast Fact

If your doctor has recommended angioplasty or cardiac surgery, seek out a cardiologist or a heart surgeon at a medical center where angioplasty and bypass surgery are frequently performed. As you might expect, research has shown that outcomes are best at the institutions with the most experience.

evidence warrants testing for aspirin resistance or altering the prescription for blood-thinning drugs accordingly.

Coronary Artery Bypass Graft (CABG) Surgery

In coronary artery bypass graft (CABG) surgery, the cardiac surgeon takes a length of blood vessel from elsewhere in the body and uses it to shunt blood around a narrowed or blocked coronary artery. The attached vessel thus permits blood to bypass the blockage so the heart muscle ordinarily supplied by that coronary artery can once again receive nourishment. About 366,000 Americans undergo CABG surgery each year. The operation can dramatically improve the quality of life and boost life expectancy for some (but not all) people with coronary artery disease.

The latest guidelines from the American College of Cardiology and the American Heart Association recommend that physicians consider CABG surgery when there is a blockage of 50 percent or more in the left main coronary artery, alone, or 70 percent or more in all three other major coronary arteries. Bypass should be considered in such circumstances even when patients have few or no symptoms of angina. According to the guidelines, a CABG procedure can also be beneficial for patients who've had angioplasty but who continue to have symptoms caused by blocked arteries, as well as for patients who've already had bypass surgery but suffer from disabling angina.

In CABG surgery, the patient is under general anesthesia, and the surgeon cuts through the breastbone to gain access to the heart. In the conventional approach to bypass surgery, the heart is usually stopped with a solution called cardioplegia so that the surgeon doesn't have to perform surgery on a heart that's constantly moving. A heart-lung machine pumps oxygen-rich blood through the patient's body, temporarily substituting for the heart. The surgeon takes a vein or an artery from another part of the patient's body and stitches it into place to reroute blood around the blocked artery.

The replacement vessel might be an internal mammary artery taken from the patient's chest wall, a radial artery from the patient's arm, or a saphenous vein taken from the leg. In any case, the artery or vein is a "spare" vessel. The patient will suffer no major ill effects because that piece of artery or vein has been removed.

If the grafted vessel is a vein from a leg or a radial artery from an arm, one end is attached to the aorta and the other is sewn onto the diseased coronary artery, beyond the blockage. When an internal mammary artery is used, the upper end is usually left attached to a large artery called the subclavian artery, and the lower open end is attached to the diseased coronary artery, beyond the blockage. Artery grafts (particularly the internal mammary artery grafts) tend to last longer than vein grafts, and the use of artery grafts has been shown to prolong life.

After the surgery is completed, the patient's heart is started again, and he or she is taken off the heart-lung machine. Most people stay in the hospital for four to five days after the operation, though within one to two days of surgery the doctor will probably ask the patient to get up and walk.

If you should undergo CABG surgery, you might also be scheduled for a cardiac-rehabilitation program, which you will attend after leaving the hospital. Cardiac rehabilitation helps you and your heart gain strength. It also teaches you heart-healthy practices that will help protect you from future heart disease, such as observing a low-fat diet and exercising regularly.

Beating-Heart Surgery

The latest innovation in CABG surgery is a procedure called off-pump bypass or beating-heart surgery (see Figure 3.3). In this

FIGURE 3.3 Beating-Heart Surgery

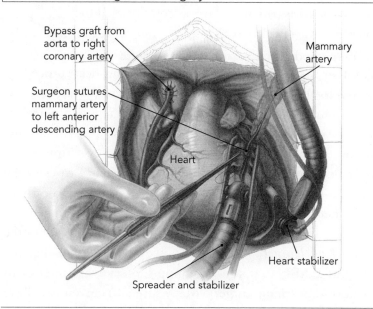

Bypass graft from aorta to right coronary artery

Mammary artery

Surgeon sutures mammary artery to left anterior descending artery

Heart

Heart stabilizer

Spreader and stabilizer

Traditional coronary artery bypass graft surgery requires the use of a heart-lung machine to circulate the blood while the heart is stopped. In "beating-heart surgery," also known as "off-pump" surgery, devices called stabilizers hold a portion of the heart still, allowing the surgeon to suture bypass vessels in place as the rest of the heart continues to beat. The advantages of this procedure include quicker recovery, reduced trauma to the heart and other organs, and possibly a lessening of memory loss and other neurological consequences.

procedure, the operating team doesn't stop the heart and place the patient on a heart-lung machine. Instead, the surgeon uses special equipment to hold the heart steady, enabling the surgeon to operate on it while it continues beating. The surgeon still splits the entire breastbone but avoids putting the patient on the heart-lung machine. Off-pump CABG is probably best suited for patients in whom the heart-lung machine may pose important complications such as neurological deficits or kidney failure.

By avoiding the heart-lung machine, off-pump CABG was also expected to lower the rate of some complications, such as memory impairment and lessened ability to concentrate. But a 2002 study in the *Journal of the American Medical Association* found that after twelve months, patients who had the off-pump procedure were as likely to have suffered memory loss and other cognitive problems as patients who had conventional bypass surgery. However, with just 281 patients, the study was too small to be definitive.

Another key question is whether the beating-heart procedure is as effective as standard coronary artery bypass graft surgery. Results from a recent study at one hospital that regularly performs this operation were encouraging. Investigators found that outcomes were very good and that they improved over time as the doctors became more experienced. By the last 174 cases in the series, one-year survival rates were excellent. But it's too early to tell whether survival rates were as good as those of patients who had conventional bypass surgery. Another paper published in the *New England Journal of Medicine*, however, suggested that the patency of CABG grafts in off-pump surgery were inferior to conventional on-pump surgery. Many surgeons currently believe that off-pump surgery should be used in selected patients to decrease the risk associated with the heart-lung machine, but should not be the first choice for most patients.

Alternative Remedies

Several natural therapies are promoted as treatments for heart disease. Some have been put to the test in scientific studies and look promising, but others have not held up to scientific scrutiny. Many such herbal remedies and alternative treatments—available in drugstores and on the Internet—remain unproved and therefore should be taken with caution. And because herbs and other nutritional supplements are not reviewed for purity or effectiveness by the FDA, you can't be sure that what you're buying is effective or even that the bottle contains the substance on the label.

If you take any herbal remedies, be sure to tell your doctor. These preparations may hinder or exaggerate the effects of prescription drugs used to manage cardiovascular disease. Indeed, heart patients are more vulnerable than most others to adverse drug interactions. Here is some information about two popular alternative remedies for heart disease. Of course, there are many others out there that I just don't have the space to cover.

Coenzyme Q10

This vitamin-like substance is found in every cell in the body but is most prevalent in tissues with high energy demands, such as the muscles of the heart. Many advocates of alternative medicine believe that it can strengthen the heartbeat by increasing the cellular fuel available to the heart muscle. And some small studies have suggested that it might help patients with angina, heart failure, or other cardiovascular problems.

But a few years ago, researchers in Australia conducted a rigorous trial that evaluated coenzyme Q10 in thirty patients with heart failure. All were taking conventional medicines, but for twelve weeks each subject also took either coenzyme Q10 or a placebo. At the end of the study, there was no change in the strength of the heartbeat as evaluated by echocardiography and cardiac catheterization. And the people who took coenzyme Q10 did not feel better or report improved ability to function.

Chelation Therapy

Chelation therapy uses infusions, or slow injections, of a chemical called ethylenediaminetetraacetic acid (EDTA). This process is sometimes used to remove toxic levels of lead, iron, or other metals from the body. (The metals exit the body via the urine.) Some experts think that the oxidation of LDL cholesterol requires interaction with such metals. The idea behind chelation for cardiovascular disease is that removing some of these metals from the bloodstream will also reduce oxidation—and this "antioxidant" effect might improve blood vessel function.

By some estimates, as many as 500,000 Americans are spending more than $3 billion per year on chelation. But little scientific research has assessed its value for heart disease. In 2000, the *American Heart Journal* published a review of small studies and concluded that chelation was ineffective for heart disease. As is the case with many alternative remedies, clinical trials are needed to prove or disprove the effectiveness of this therapy. A large trial conducted by the National Institutes of Health will do just that. Scheduled to end in 2008, the study will determine whether chelation therapy is safe for people who have heart disease and whether it decreases the chances of another heart attack.

Choose the Treatment That's Right for You

Because of the different degrees of heart disease and its different causes, no one treatment style will suit all. For some, diet and exercise will work well enough that no medication is needed. For others, lifestyle changes will have to be supplemented with a medication or two. And for still others, their heart disease is so serious that they need surgery to correct it. It's important to remember that changing your diet, exercise, and smoking habits are important ways to keep heart disease at bay, even if you're on other treatments as well.

CHAPTER 4

Risk Factors for Heart Disease

Over the past several decades, many careful studies have identified personal traits and habits that increase the risk of developing heart disease. Some of these risk factors are stronger than others; some are under your control, and some are beyond it. The impacts of some risk factors have been well documented, while others are just emerging. No matter which risk factors you have, it's important to remember that they reinforce one another: the more you have, the greater your chances of developing heart disease.

Unavoidable Risk Factors

There are some things that raise your risk for heart disease that you cannot control, but you can reduce their impact by working on the many avoidable risk factors discussed later in this chapter.

Age

Heart disease becomes more prevalent with age. Simply put, older people have more heart attacks than younger people do. About 80 percent of people who die from heart attacks are over age sixty-five. In America, the risk for heart attack begins to accelerate in men after they reach the age of forty-five and in women after age fifty-five.

Gender

In younger people, gender is a major predictor of risk. Before age sixty, one in five American men—but only one in seventeen women—will have had a coronary event. The naturally produced female hormone, estrogen, may be one of the reasons for this gender difference. But after a woman goes through menopause, this advantage is lost. Beyond age sixty, equality is the rule, and coronary artery disease kills 25 percent of women and men alike. In the United States, heart disease is the leading killer of both women and men.

However, there are a few concerns that pertain only to women. First, although the death rate from heart disease has declined for both genders, it is declining in women less rapidly than in men. Currently, 38 percent of women who've had heart attacks die within a year, compared with 25 percent of men.

Second, most women who die suddenly from coronary artery disease don't have typical warning symptoms. Some may have had symptoms that they didn't recognize as signs of heart attack because women's symptoms often differ from men's (see Chapter 2 for more on this). Sometimes doctors pay less attention to women's symptoms than they do to men's because they know that younger women are less likely to develop heart disease. Academic medical centers like the one where I practice are spending more time educating young doctors to pay attention to women's heart symptoms so that those symptoms are not dismissed as a less serious complaint, such as heartburn.

Given these issues, what should women do? Perhaps most important, they need to focus on prevention. For many years, doctors recommended hormone replacement therapy to women who were entering menopause because of evidence that it reduced the risk for heart disease as well as osteoporosis. But the heart-protective benefits of HRT have come under fire. Clinical trials have found that women with heart disease who take HRT do not have fewer heart attacks than women who don't take it. In fact, it actually slightly raises the risk of heart disease in both healthy women and women who have had previous episodes of athero-sclerotic heart trouble.

It's a different story for men and heart disease. While female hormones appear to provide some heart-protective benefits—at least for younger women—male hormones may contribute to heart disease in five ways:

- Boosting LDL and lowering HDL
- Promoting the accumulation of abdominal fat, which can lead to high triglyceride levels and diabetes
- Increasing the number of red blood cells and activating the clotting system
- Triggering spasms that narrow arteries
- Enlarging and possibly damaging heart muscle cells

Scientists have discovered some of these effects after giving testos-terone to laboratory animals. It will take time for researchers to determine whether a normal amount of testosterone increases a man's risk for heart disease. Testosterone isn't all bad for the heart—it appears to reduce the level of one newly identified car-diac risk factor, lipoprotein(a).

Family History

Coronary artery disease runs in families. While families share genes, they also share lifestyles such as smoking, diet, inactivity, or stress. Which is to blame, genetics or lifestyle? Both.

About a dozen genetic abnormalities have been identified that seem to increase the risk for different kinds of heart problems. For instance, defects in nine different genes can cause cardiomyopa-thy, a form of heart failure in which the heart is unable to pump blood efficiently. In 2002, researchers reported in the journal *Cir-culation* that a variant of a gene called the peroxisome proliferator alpha may predispose people to develop a dangerously enlarged heart after intensive exercise or as a side effect of high blood pres-

Keeping Track of Your Family Tree

It can be hard to keep track of your own medical history, let alone your family members'. Here are some tips:

- Concentrate on your immediate family first. Though it can be helpful to recognize patterns that go back generations, your risk for a disease generally increases the most if a first-degree relative (your parents, siblings, or children) has it.
- Explain to your family how important it is to know each other's medical histories. Ask your family members to write down any conditions they've been treated for, the date, how old they were at the time, and any pertinent details (such as exactly how high your brother's cholesterol was).
- Offer to gather the information into one place and make copies for everyone. You can use the chart in Figure 4.1 to get started.

sure. Genetic research is in its infancy, but the hope is that genetic testing will enable doctors to identify people at high risk for heart problems and perhaps help them avoid heart disease with preventive treatment.

But, in any case, genes are not the final word in determining who will develop heart disease. Researchers for the Framingham Heart Study, a long-term observational study that has tracked the health of more than five thousand people in a Massachusetts town since the late 1940s, estimate that having a family history of heart disease increases an individual's risk by about 25 percent. To put this in perspective, smoking increases your risk ten times this rate. Moreover, not every family history is equally worrisome; it takes a strong history (for example, a father or brother afflicted before age fifty-five or a mother or sister stricken before age sixty-five) to increase your risk.

Many people with a family history of coronary artery disease have early signs of the disease. The American Heart Association

FIGURE 4.1 Family Medical History Chart

Family Member	Condition(s)	Date	Age	Comments
Mother				
Father				
Siblings				
Children				
Other				

now recommends that everyone undergo cholesterol profile screenings for heart disease at age twenty. If you have a family history, it's vital for you to address risk factors like high blood pressure and elevated cholesterol, and to adopt a heart-healthy lifestyle in your youth.

Avoidable Risk Factors

Fortunately, most of the risk factors for coronary artery disease can be partially or totally addressed. Many are unhealthy habits, such as smoking and lack of exercise. Others, such as high blood cholesterol and obesity, can be partly or mostly due to poor diet choices, although genetic susceptibilities can dramatically influence the response to those choices. Some are treatable illnesses such as depression and high blood pressure. And still others are circumstances, such as social isolation and stress, that can be mitigated to some degree. By addressing the risk factors that you have some control over, it's possible to reduce your vulnerability to coronary artery disease by a third or more.

Unfavorable Cholesterol Levels

Elevated levels of total blood cholesterol, in the higher ranges of what one typically sees in a medical practice, increase heart attack rates 2.4 times, which is the very reason high cholesterol should be lowered. In the next chapter, I'll go over exactly which cholesterol levels are unfavorable.

Tobacco Exposure

Everyone knows that smoking is a major health hazard: it's the leading preventable cause of death in the United States. But some people may be surprised to learn that smoking is also the most potent cardiac risk factor, increasing risk by 250 percent. Another surprise: exposure to secondhand smoke is also a major cardiac risk factor, which is why passive smoking is the nation's third-leading preventable cause of death. (Alcohol is the second.)

In all, smoking accounts for 20 percent of all deaths from coronary artery disease. But within a year of quitting, smokers can cut this risk in half. Within two years, the cardiovascular risk for a former smoker is very close to that of a person who never smoked. Because smoking probably contributes to blood vessel inflammation, removing that irritant should slow the inflammatory process, resulting in a quick drop in heart disease risk.

I see a lot of patients who know they should quit smoking, but they're not sure how. The best approach is two-pronged: use medicine, and get counseling and support.

Easing the craving for nicotine is a key part of stopping smoking. Several aids can help with this (see Table 4.1). Nicotine patches, gum, lozenges, nasal spray, and cigarette-shaped inhalers deliver enough nicotine to satisfy the body without the tar, carbon monoxide, and other harmful chemicals found in cigarette smoke. An antidepressant known as bupropion (Zyban, Wellbutrin) also alleviates the symptoms of nicotine withdrawal, even in people who aren't depressed. Combining bupropion and nicotine replacement may work the best of all.

Nicotine replacement is safe, even after a heart attack, and it's much safer than continued smoking. These products don't increase the clotting potential of blood or damage the fragile but important lining of blood vessels, as smoking does.

Nicotine replacement often isn't enough on its own. Counseling and social support can help you break your "smoking cues," the things you link to lighting up, like drinking coffee or finishing a big meal. You can get counseling one-on-one at a support group run by a hospital or local department of health, via the phone, or online. (Some options are listed in the Resources section.)

Remember that quitting smoking is a huge change, so it might take you a few tries to get off cigarettes for good. If you slip by having a cigarette or two after your quit date, try to figure out what went wrong and how to fix it the next time. Don't convince yourself that as long as you had one, you may as well have another, and another. . . . The same holds true if you return to your old

TABLE 4.1 Stop-Smoking Aids

Aid	Advantages	Disadvantages	Dosage	Availability, Cost
Nicotine patch	Gives a stable level of nicotine in the blood for 16–24 hours; easy to use	Takes 2–4 hours to hit peak level; user can't adjust dose to meet cravings	One 7 mg, 14 mg, or 21 mg patch a day	Prescription and over the counter, $4 a day
Nicotine gum	Rapid rise in blood level of nicotine; user can control dose to respond to cravings; oral substitute for cigarette	Must be chewed properly to get nicotine and avoid upset stomach; can cause mouth soreness or indigestion	Up to 24 pieces a day	Over the counter, $6–$7 a day
Nicotine inhaler	Rapid rise in blood level of nicotine; user controls the dose; hand-to-mouth substitute for smoking	Requires frequent puffs; can irritate the mouth and throat	6–16 cartridges a day	Prescription only, $5–$15 a day
Nicotine nasal spray	Offers the quickest increase in blood nicotine levels; user controls the dose	Can irritate the nose and throat; can cause cough	8–40 sprays a day	Prescription only, $4–$15 a day
Nicotine lozenge	User controls the dose; oral substitute for smoking	Can cause sore mouth, indigestion, hiccups	10–16 lozenges a day	Over the counter, $5–$9 a day
Bupropion (Wellbutrin, Zyban)	Easy to use; no nicotine involved	Can cause insomnia, dry mouth, agitation; shouldn't be used by anyone with a seizure or eating disorder	Start 1–2 weeks before quit date; 2 times a day	Prescription only; about $3 a day
Counseling	Helpful for long-term cessation	Requires commitment of time and possibly money	Once a week or more often if needed	Ranges from free to expensive (private counseling)

Source: "Let the Butt Stop Here," *Harvard Heart Letter*, October 2003, page 5.

What's Your Blood Pressure?

There is no single normal blood pressure; instead, blood pressure readings range from ideal at the low end, to acceptable in the middle, and abnormally high at the top. Table 4.2 shows the standard levels for people age eighteen and above. If your blood pressure is high on the first reading, have it taken again a few minutes later. It may have been temporarily elevated because of stress over running late for the appointment (or your doctor running way behind in the appointment schedule) or exertion from climbing the stairs to the office.

TABLE 4.2 Blood Pressure Ranges

Category	Systolic Blood Pressure (mm Hg)		Diastolic Blood Pressure (mm Hg)
Normal (optimal)	less than 120	and	less than 80
Prehypertension	120–139	or	80–89
Stage 1 hypertension	140–159	or	90–99
Stage 2 hypertension	160 or higher	or	100 or higher

smoking habit. You may have to quit a few times. Not succeeding may just mean you need more help.

High Blood Pressure

High blood pressure (or hypertension) is nearly as dangerous as high cholesterol. People with this condition are more than twice as likely to suffer a heart attack as those with normal blood pressure are. Because fifty million Americans have hypertension, it's a major cause of atherosclerosis, to say nothing of the death and disability that it brings about through stroke and other hypertensive diseases such as kidney failure.

Your blood pressure reading has two parts, the systolic blood pressure (the top number) and the diastolic blood pressure (the bottom number). The systolic number represents the pressure while the heart is beating, and the diastolic number represents the pressure when the heart is refilling with blood between beats.

To determine if you have high blood pressure, look up your numbers in Table 4.2. What if your systolic blood pressure is high but your diastolic is not, or vice versa? Use the higher category to determine your status. For example, if your blood pressure is 162/85 millimeters of mercury (mm Hg) you have Stage 2 hypertension.

The lower your blood pressure, the lower your risk for heart attack, stroke, kidney disease, and premature death. With this in mind, aim for a blood pressure of less than 140/90 mm Hg. But people with cardiovascular disease (or other conditions that increase the risk of cardiovascular disease) should aim for an even lower level, of no more than 135/85 mm Hg and, ideally, 120/80 mm Hg or less.

Because high blood pressure usually begins gradually between ages twenty and fifty, all adults should have their blood pressure checked regularly. Blood pressure checks every three years usually suffice for people with normal or optimal levels. But people with elevated blood pressure need more frequent measurement—at least once a year for those with high-normal blood pressure. People who are at increased risk of developing high blood pressure (including African-Americans, relatives of people with hypertension, and patients with kidney disease) should also have their blood pressure checked at least once a year, even if their own numbers are normal.

If you have high blood pressure, there are medications you can take and lifestyle changes you can make. Many of the things that help prevent heart disease confer part of their benefit by lowering blood pressure. Regular exercise and weight loss are prime examples. Smoking cessation, moderate alcohol use, stress reduction, and a low-fat, high-fiber, vitamin-rich diet may also help control blood pressure. An eating plan called Dietary Approaches to Stop Hypertension (DASH) has proved effective in reducing high blood pressure. The DASH diet is rich in fruits, vegetables, and low-fat dairy products and low in saturated fats. It's particularly effective if you also restrict the amount of salt you eat. No matter what treatment you're on, make sure your doctor monitors you closely to ensure that you get good results.

The benefits of blood pressure control are substantial; just a 1 mm Hg decline in diastolic blood pressure can reduce your cardiac risk by 2 percent to 3 percent. Although diastolic blood pressure was previously considered most important, experts now understand that reducing the systolic blood pressure can be just as helpful. Because blood pressure tends to rise with age, even people in the "normal" and "optimal" ranges should consider taking steps to keep their blood pressure there.

Diabetes

Diabetes has long been recognized as a major risk factor for heart disease, but we now have evidence that an otherwise-healthy middle-aged individual with diabetes is just as likely to have a first heart attack as a nondiabetic person who has already suffered a heart attack is to have a second coronary event. Because we have always treated individuals who have had a previous heart attack very aggressively—because this is one of the biggest predictors of future coronary events—we have begun to do the same thing in our diabetic patients. To put some specific numbers to the magnitude of this risk, research has shown that people with diabetes have a 15 percent to 25 percent chance of developing serious heart problems over a ten-year period. Even more sobering, a person with diabetes who has a heart attack is twice as likely to die from it as a person without diabetes would be. Two-thirds of people with diabetes die of some form of heart or blood vessel disease.

Although there's a genetic component to diabetes, the most common form of the disease, type 2 diabetes (formerly known as adult-onset diabetes), can often be controlled or even prevented by weight loss, regular aerobic exercise, and diet. For anyone with diabetes, good blood sugar control is a major goal of medical therapy. Fasting blood sugar levels above 140 mg/dL indicate a need for additional treatment. Studies are currently under way to determine if better blood sugar control in diabetics will reduce their risk for heart disease (we don't know that for sure yet), but it has been clearly shown to prevent complications involving the kidney and eyes.

If you have diabetes, be particularly careful to reduce your other heart disease risk factors.

Obesity

Because obesity is so closely linked to high blood pressure, unfavorable cholesterol levels, lack of exercise, and diabetes, it took scientists a long time to figure out whether obesity itself is an independent cardiac risk factor. Experts now agree that it is. Excess weight increases your risk for heart disease regardless of these other conditions. All forms of obesity are bad for your health, but excessive upper-body fat (an apple-shaped body) is more dangerous to the heart than lower-body obesity (the pear shape). In other words, fat stored at or above your waistline is worse than fat in your hips and thighs.

Your body mass index (BMI), which takes both height and weight into consideration, provides an accurate reflection of your body fat. (Use Table 4.3 to calculate your BMI.) You should aim for a BMI of between 18.5 and 24, the range that's considered normal. A BMI between 25 and 29 is considered overweight, and a value of 30 or higher is defined as obese.

You should also keep an eye on your waist measurement, which is an indication of your body-fat level. As people grow older, for example, their waist size often increases, though the scale tells them they weigh the same as they did the previous year. That's because people tend to lose muscle mass as they age, but if they gain enough fat, they maintain the same weight.

Unfortunately, it's much easier to diagnose obesity than to correct it. But because maintaining a healthy body weight can reduce cardiac risk by 35 percent to 55 percent, it's an important goal. Rather than focusing on the weight itself, it's best to work toward

What's My BMI?

To estimate your body mass index (BMI), first identify your weight (to the nearest ten pounds) in the top row of Table 4.3. Next, move your finger down the column below that weight until you come to the row that represents your height. The number at the intersection of your height and weight is your BMI.

TABLE 4.3 Body Mass Index

Height	Weight															
	100	110	120	130	140	150	160	170	180	190	200	210	220	230	240	250
5'0"	20	21	23	25	27	29	31	33	35	37	39	41	43	45	47	49
5'1"	19	21	23	25	26	28	30	32	34	36	38	40	42	43	45	47
5'2"	18	20	22	24	26	27	29	31	33	35	37	38	40	42	44	46
5'3"	18	19	21	23	25	27	28	30	32	34	35	37	39	41	43	44
5'4"	17	19	21	22	24	26	27	29	31	33	34	36	38	39	41	43
5'5"	17	18	20	22	23	25	27	28	30	32	33	35	37	38	40	42
5'6"	16	18	19	21	23	24	26	27	29	31	32	34	36	37	39	40
5'7"	16	17	19	20	22	23	25	27	28	30	31	33	34	36	38	39
5'8"	15	17	18	20	21	23	24	26	27	29	30	32	33	35	36	38
5'9"	15	16	18	19	21	22	24	25	27	28	30	31	32	34	35	37
5'10"	14	16	17	19	20	22	23	24	26	27	29	30	32	33	34	36
5'11"	14	15	17	18	20	21	22	24	25	26	27	28	30	32	33	35
6'0"	14	15	16	18	19	20	22	23	24	26	27	28	30	31	33	34
6'1"	13	15	16	17	18	20	21	22	24	25	26	28	29	30	32	33
6'2"	13	14	15	17	18	19	21	22	23	24	26	27	28	30	31	32
6'3"	12	14	15	16	17	19	20	21	22	24	25	26	27	29	30	31
6'4"	12	13	15	16	17	18	19	21	22	23	24	26	27	28	29	30

BMI Interpretation

Under 18.5	Underweight
18.5–24	Normal
25–29	Overweight
30 and above	Obese

Anger: What's Your Score?

Several studies have demonstrated that people with a low threshold for anger have a greater probability of high blood pressure and heart disease. When compared with calmer people, these individuals experience rage and fury more often, more intensely, and for longer periods of time.

Information from a long-term epidemiological study done at Duke University called Atherosclerosis Risk in Communities (ARIC) offers some perspective on the relative importance of this risk factor. As part of the investigation, subjects were asked to complete the Spielberger State-Trait Anger Expression Inventory, a questionnaire used by psychologists to assess how anger prone a person is. Subjects had to respond to these ten statements by answering: Almost Never = 1, Sometimes = 2, Often = 3, and Almost Always = 4. The overall anger score is calculated by adding together the ratings for each statement.

- I am quick-tempered.
- I have a fiery temper.
- I am a hotheaded person.
- I get angry when I am slowed down by others' mistakes.

a heart-healthy lifestyle featuring a lot of aerobic exercise and a diet low in saturated and trans fats. It's no accident that this program works well for the waist as well as the heart.

Diet

When it comes to heart disease risk, you are what you eat. A poor diet—one high in saturated fat, trans-fatty acids (partially hydrogenated fats or oils), cholesterol, refined carbohydrates, and calories—can promote heart disease. However, a healthy diet—one low in these substances and high in fruits, vegetables, and grains—can help protect you against it. Diet exerts tremendous influence on many of the risk factors for heart disease—not just choles-

- I feel annoyed when I am not given recognition for doing good work.
- I fly off the handle.
- When I get angry, I say nasty things.
- It makes me furious when I am criticized in front of others.
- When I get frustrated, I feel like hitting someone.
- I feel infuriated when I do a good job and get a poor evaluation.

Scoring: 22–40 = high anger; 15–21 = moderate anger; 10–14 = low anger

In the Duke study, the higher a person's anger score, the greater the risk of developing coronary artery disease during the seventy-two-month follow-up period. The findings don't prove that anger causes heart problems or that measures to control anger will help anyone live longer. But they do suggest a close relationship between psychological and cardiovascular health. If you take the quiz and get a high anger score, go to pages 66–67 for tips on how to control your anger.

terol—including high blood pressure, diabetes, and obesity. This is such an important topic that I've devoted a large section of Chapter 6 to developing and sticking with a heart-healthy, cholesterol-lowering diet plan.

Psychological Factors

The links between the heart and mind are harder to quantify than those between the heart and the waistline, but most authorities think that psychological factors are—literally—heartfelt and can contribute to cardiac risk. Psychological stress, anger, social isolation, and depression are often related—people who have one commonly have another. Evidence suggests that such problems

Are You Depressed?

Identifying the symptoms of depression can be a useful first step toward gaining a deeper understanding of how depression, bipolar disorder, or the long-lasting low-level depression called dysthymia (pronounced dis-THIGH-me-a) affects you. It may help you open a discussion with a doctor or therapist, too.

Be aware, however, that self-tests like this one cannot diagnose depression or any other mental illness. Even if they could, it's easy to dismiss or overlook symptoms in yourself. It may help to have a friend or relative go over this checklist with you. Also, remember that your feelings count far more than the number of check marks you make. If you think you are depressed or if you have other concerns or questions after taking this test, talk with your doctor or therapist.

Depression Checklist

Start by checking off any symptoms of depression that you have had for two weeks or longer. Focus on symptoms that have been present almost every day for most of the day. (The exception is the item regarding thoughts of suicide or suicide attempts. A check mark there warrants an immediate call to the doctor.) Then look at the key that follows the list.

☐ I feel sad or irritable.

☐ I have lost interest in activities I used to enjoy.

☐ I'm eating much less than I usually do and have lost weight, or I'm eating much more than I usually do and have gained weight.

can increase the risk for coronary artery disease and the risk of dying after a heart attack.

Psychological stress can raise blood pressure, reduce blood flow to the heart, decrease the heart's pumping ability, trigger abnormal pumping rhythms, and activate the blood's clotting system. Even a less extreme stressor, such as loneliness, seems to influence

☐ I am sleeping much less or more than I usually do.

☐ I have no energy or feel tired much of the time.

☐ I feel anxious and can't seem to sit still.

☐ I feel guilty or worthless.

☐ I have trouble concentrating or find it hard to make decisions.

☐ I have recurring thoughts about death or suicide, I have a suicide plan, or I have tried to commit suicide.

Now think about other symptoms you have noticed during this time:

☐ I feel hopeless.

☐ I have lost interest in sex, including fantasies.

☐ I have headaches, aches and pains, digestive troubles, or other physical symptoms.

Scoring the Test

If you checked a total of five or more statements on the depression checklist, including at least one of the first two statements, you may be suffering from an episode of major depression. If you checked fewer statements, including at least one of the first two statements, you may be suffering from a milder form of depression or dysthymia. Either way, your doctor may be able to recommend treatments to help.

blood pressure, according to a 2002 study in the journal *Psychosomatic Medicine*. When researchers measured the blood pressure of eighty-nine students during a stressful test-taking experiment, those who had reported that they were lonely had increased blood pressure due to greater constriction of their arteries, which can be harmful in the long term. Those who weren't lonely had increased blood pressure due to increased cardiac output (more blood pumped out by the heart), a more normal stress response.

Interestingly, it's the way you react to stress rather than the stress itself that can be dangerous to your heart. Some people take life's stresses in stride, while others are more likely to become upset and angry. People who tend to be angry by temperament have strong emotional reactions when under stress and often overreact in ordinary circumstances as well. A 2001 study in the *American Journal of Epidemiology* found that having a fiery personality was as strong a risk factor for heart disease as high blood pressure.

The study, which included 12,990 middle-aged men and women, assessed the participants' overall health and used a psychological questionnaire to identify those with angry temperaments. Over the next three to six years, people who had angry temperaments had a risk for heart disease two and a half times greater than that of their more laid-back counterparts. The increase in risk was comparable to that of having high blood pressure.

It's important to note that it's very hard to conduct stress studies well. Measurements of anxiety and temperament are simply much harder to quantify than cholesterol level or body weight. Measurement of stress levels often involves some subjective judgment on the part of the study participant or the researcher. That's not to say that the evidence on stress's effect on your heart (or other body parts) is wrong, but it is the kind of evidence that may be refined as better research tools make it possible to evaluate human psychology with greater precision.

As for depression, a study of 5,007 women and 2,886 men found that depressed women had a 73 percent greater risk of developing coronary artery disease than women who weren't depressed—and that depressed men were 71 percent more likely to develop coronary artery disease than men who weren't depressed. Although the depressed women weren't at an increased risk of dying from heart disease, the depressed men were 2.3 times more likely to die from it than men who weren't depressed.

Other studies have shown that lingering depression is a strong predictor of second heart attacks.

The relationship between depression and heart disease is a two-way street. Depression may not only promote but also be a product of heart attack. For as many as a third of people, depression follows a heart attack. Whether you've had a heart attack or not, if you feel depressed, tell your doctor. Depression can be treated successfully with antidepressants, psychosocial therapy, or both. Treating depression can make you feel better, and studies are under way to see whether effective treatment for depression can prevent or reverse heart problems or extend life.

A study from Canada showed that strong social support blunts the relationship between depression and the risk of dying after a heart attack. It could be that social ties reduce the risk of dying by helping to relieve depression. But another benefit could be purely practical: people with strong social support have more friends and relatives to encourage them to take their medications, exercise, and lose weight.

Some careful studies suggest that stress-reduction techniques may help lower blood pressure and reduce the risk for recurrent heart attacks. Some or all of the following approaches can help:

- **Physical exercise.** Aerobic exercise can actually dissipate stress and help control depression. Vigorous exercise stimulates the body's production of natural chemicals that elevate mood and diminish pain.
- **Behavioral changes.** You can reduce your stress level by identifying the tasks, situations, and relationships that cause you undue stress and then modifying them as best you can. For example, if you have too much to do in too little time, set realistic goals and establish priorities. Let the least important items go for now. If, on the other hand, you feel stressed by a lack of focus or challenge in your life, look for new activities and interests to help you get out of a rut. Whatever the cause of your stress, find constructive ways to

Relaxation Techniques

Breath Focus

What Is It? Focusing on slow, deep breathing and gently disengaging the mind from distracting thoughts and sensations

Especially Beneficial: If you have an eating disorder or tend to hold in your stomach (may help you focus on your body in healthier ways)

May Not Be Suitable: If you have health problems that make breathing difficult, such as respiratory ailments or congestive heart failure

Progressive Muscle Relaxation

What Is It? Tensing and relaxing all the muscles of the body from head to toe in a progressive sequence

Especially Beneficial: At times when your mind is racing or if you have trouble sensing and releasing tension

May Not Be Suitable: If you have an eating disorder or have had recent surgery that affects body image or if you have a condition that makes tensing the body especially uncomfortable

Mindfulness Meditation

What Is It? Breathing deeply while staying in the moment by deliberately focusing on thoughts and sensations that arise during the meditation session

Especially Beneficial: If racing thoughts make other forms of meditation difficult

May Not Be Suitable: If you find it too hard to commit the thirty to forty-five minutes suggested

reduce or eliminate it. Don't rely on alcohol, nicotine, or drugs to solve problems.

- **Autoregulation techniques.** Experiment with deep breathing, progressive muscular relaxation, or meditation. By learning to relax your body, you may find that you can relax your mind.

- **Mindfulness.** You can also incorporate mindfulness, the practice of being aware of your thoughts and feelings, in everyday life. Try the following:

  1. Make something that occurs several times a day, such as answering the phone or buckling your seat belt, a reminder to return to the present—that is, think about what you're doing and observe yourself doing it.

  2. Pay attention to your breathing or your environment when you stop at red lights.

  3. Before you go to sleep and when you awaken, take some "mindful" breaths. Instead of allowing your mind to wander over the day's concerns, direct your attention to your breathing. Feel its effects on your nostrils, lungs, and abdomen. Try to think of nothing else.

  4. If the present moment involves stress—perhaps you're about to speak in public or undergo a medical test— observe your thoughts and emotions and how they affect your body.

  5. Find a task you usually do impatiently or unconsciously (standing in line or brushing your teeth, for example), and really pay attention to what's going on.

- **Counseling or psychotherapy.** Seek help from a mental health professional, such as a psychologist, social worker, or psychiatrist. Support groups and stress-management classes can also help.

- **Anger management.** At least two studies have shown that people with heart disease can curb their anger by getting regular exercise or counseling. The studies also found that reducing anger and hostility levels could decrease

How to Manage Your Anger

The following tips may help you control your anger:

- **Use the relaxation tools** on page 64. They can help with managing not only stress but anger as well.
- **Change the way you think.** When you're angry, your inner voice may curse or use colorful terms that exaggerate or dramatize the situation. This can serve to justify your anger. Try to replace these thoughts with more rational ones. So if your car breaks down, instead of saying to yourself, "This @#$! thing never works right! This delay is going to ruin everything!" tell yourself that it's understandable that you're frustrated but that getting angry isn't going to fix the car.
- **Don't demand.** Angry people tend to demand things. Watch how often you say to yourself, "I must have" or "I demand." Change your thoughts to "I would like." Remember that getting angry is not going to make you feel better—in fact, it'll probably do the opposite.
- **Get logical.** Even when anger is justified, the level or direction can often become irrational. So use cold hard logic on yourself.

participants' risk factors for heart disease and make them feel better, as well as forestall the recurrence of heart attacks. It's not known whether anger management can prevent heart disease.

Emerging Risk Factors

You may have heard about new tests such as those that measure homocysteine or C-reactive protein levels (see page 68) that can estimate risk for heart disease. There are four critical questions that must be answered about any new risk factor before it can be recommended that the general population get screened for it:

For example, remind yourself that the world is not "out to get you," that you're just experiencing some of the downs of daily life. Do this each time you feel anger taking hold of you, and it'll help you get a more balanced perspective.

- **Laugh.** Silly humor can help defuse rage in a number of ways. You may want to exaggerate the situation in your mind until it becomes so ludicrous it's funny. For example, if you think the world is out to get you, picture a globe running down the street, giving you flat tires, directing you to the slow line at the grocery store, or causing traffic jams just for you.
- **Try something new.** If you get angry every morning and every evening because of rush hour traffic, map out a different route. Maybe one that takes you a little longer but that is scenic or less congested would help.

Adapted from information from the American Psychological Association

1. Is there an accurate laboratory test for the risk factor?
2. Will measurement of the risk factor provide additional information beyond what can be obtained by measuring already established risk factors?
3. Will treatment of the risk factor, or use of the information it provides to treat other risks, lead to a reduction in mortality, heart attacks, or strokes?
4. Does the risk factor predict risk in the population in which it is going to be used? For example, it is possible that risk in individuals who have already had a heart attack will not prove very useful in predicting risk in individuals who have never had a heart attack.

As of this writing, the following risk factors don't meet all four of these criteria, and so I don't generally recommend testing for them *except* in these circumstances:

- You don't have any symptoms or high levels of conventional risk factors, but you do have a strong family history of CVD.
- You have early CVD without high levels of conventional risk factors.
- You have aggressive or recurrent CVD despite controlling the conventional risk factors.

Here are some of the emerging risk factors getting the most attention in the medical journals.

C-Reactive Protein (CRP)

Inflammation is the body's protective response to injury, infection, or allergy. But when inflammation occurs in coronary arteries—in response to damage inflicted by modified LDL cholesterol—it can set the stage for atherosclerosis.

C-reactive protein is a by-product of inflammation that shows up in a simple blood test. In 1997, Harvard researchers reported in the *New England Journal of Medicine* that elevated levels of CRP were a predictor of heart attacks. Healthy, middle-aged men with the highest C-reactive protein levels were nearly three times as likely to have a heart attack as those with the lowest levels. In 1998, results from the Harvard Women's Health Study showed that CRP predicts heart disease in women as well. A study done in 2004 that looked at the CRP levels of almost 6,500 people with and without heart disease found that the level did predict coronary heart disease events, but this study found it to be a less powerful predictor than cholesterol or smoking risks. This is a fairly common pattern in medical studies, where the initial reports suggest a very powerful effect and then later, larger studies find something a little more modest.

Studies have also shown that people who are obese tend to have high levels of CRP. Some exciting recent work suggests that as people gain weight, their fat tissue becomes infiltrated with inflammatory cells, which may be responsible for generating the signals that lead to elevated C-reactive protein levels. Fortunately, losing weight can reduce those levels. A 2002 study in the journal *Circulation* followed sixty-one obese postmenopausal women, twenty-five of whom participated in a weight-loss program. After thirteen months, the women had lost an average of thirty-three pounds and reduced their C-reactive protein levels by 32 percent, from 3.06 micrograms per milliliter (mcg/mL) to 1.63 mcg/mL. The more weight a woman lost, the more her CRP level declined.

CRP has almost all the elements necessary to join the fight against heart disease. It's effective at predicting heart disease risk. Testing for it isn't expensive. CRP levels aren't influenced by food, nor do they vary during the course of the day. And they can be modified. Losing weight can lower CRP. So can taking a cholesterol-lowering statin drug.

But a key piece of the puzzle is missing in our understanding of CRP. No one knows whether lowering CRP levels actually makes a difference. It is possible that CRP is simply a marker or stand-in for one of the *real* culprits behind atherosclerosis. In other words, levels of CRP go up when atherosclerosis gets worse, but CRP may only go up with that worsening, not cause it. Lowering CRP levels could then be like treating measles by covering the skin rash with makeup. While very recent scientific evidence has begun to suggest a direct role for CRP in atherosclerosis, it is still too soon to declare that relationship proved.

A four-year study started in 2003 by Harvard researchers is currently under way to determine if the lowering of CRP by statins can be separated from the effect on LDL cholesterol levels. The researchers plan to enroll fifteen thousand healthy men and women with normal LDL and high CRP. Half will take rosuvastatin and half will take a placebo. If there is a reduction in CRP levels in those with normal LDL and that is associated with a reduction in coronary events, the case for CRP will be strengthened considerably.

Another potential problem with the use of CRP levels is that they can be elevated in people with any sort of infection or other chronic inflammatory condition (such as rheumatoid arthritis), not just inflammation in the coronary arteries. While this makes the test not useful in such a patient, the real problem would come if a doctor and patient weren't aware of another inflammatory cause and incorrectly blamed the high CRP level on heart disease.

Until we know more about what high and low CRP levels really mean, not everyone needs to have this test. I advise my patients according to the following guidelines for CRP testing:

- **Don't bother** if you are already being treated very aggressively for heart disease or high cholesterol. The intervention we use for elevated CRP levels currently is treatment with the statin class of drugs. If you are already receiving that treatment, the results of a CRP test aren't likely to change how you and your doctor manage your condition. If you have arthritis, inflammatory bowel disease, or some other condition that causes inflammation and thus elevates CRP, the test for this protein might not tell you much about your future chances of developing heart disease.
- **Think about it** if your cholesterol levels are acceptable but you have other signs that heart trouble could be in your future, like a family history of heart disease, high blood pressure, or diabetes. Also, if you and your doctor are debating a change in your treatment plan, the CRP might be useful in tipping the balance in favor of moving in one direction or another.

If you get tested and find you have a high CRP level (the following chart defines what's high), pay extra attention to heart-healthy habits. Losing weight, stopping smoking, and exercising all lower CRP—and help with many other risk factors for heart disease. I also suggest to patients that they take a daily aspirin, because some studies have shown that this approach may offer protection against heart attack in people with high CRP, and we already know that taking aspirin can be helpful in preventing the clots that block arteries during a heart attack.

Some physicians have begun to prescribe statins to patients with high CRP levels, even when their LDL cholesterol levels are in the desirable range. While I don't yet subscribe to that approach (the ongoing Harvard study should answer this question in the near future), I do often try to drive LDL cholesterol levels down below current guideline targets with statin therapy, and that approach can mimic the strategy of specifically targeting inflammation in people who are already at target LDL levels.

CRP Level	Cardiovascular Risk
Below 1 mg/dL	Low
1–3 mg/dL	Moderate
Above 3 mg/dL	High (about twice the risk as someone with a CRP below 1)

Lipoprotein(a)

Although we talk almost exclusively about two lipoproteins, LDL and HDL, there are actually many others. Lipoprotein(a), which is often abbreviated as Lp(a) (pronounced el-pee-little-a), is a molecule of LDL cholesterol with an extra protein attached. Lp(a) consists of a molecule of LDL linked to a sugar-coated protein that may keep the body's natural clot-busters from doing their job. If so, high levels of Lp(a) could contribute to heart attacks.

What determines your Lp(a) level? It depends far more on genetic factors than on lifestyle. Cardiologists aren't sure what elevated Lp(a) means in terms of cardiovascular risk. Some studies show a connection between high Lp(a) and increased risk for heart disease and stroke. Others don't. One thing seems clear: high levels are worrisome in people with high LDL. Among those with normal cholesterol, Lp(a) might be important when HDL levels are low.

Homocysteine Measurement: A Fallen Star?

While early studies suggested that elevated blood levels of the amino acid homocysteine may be a major risk factor for heart disease, new studies are pushing this risk factor out of the picture. In 1992, the U.S. Physicians' Health Study reported that people with elevated homocysteine levels were nearly three times as likely to have a heart attack as those with lower levels, even after taking other risk factors into account. And this finding is by no means isolated. Since 1984, dozens of studies have reported a link between high levels of homocysteine and severe atherosclerosis involving arteries of the heart, brain, or legs. And some studies conclude that even modest increases in homocysteine are associated with higher risks of heart disease. These risks are of the same magnitude as seen with smoking or elevated levels of LDL cholesterol.

However, the first trial to measure the effect of lowering someone's homocysteine levels on stroke prevention was published in the February 4, 2004, issue of the *Journal of the American Medical Association*. In this study, two groups of patients who had had a stroke were randomly assigned to get either a high- or low-

In one major study, for example, the risk for a heart attack or sudden death was almost three times higher among men with Lp(a) levels of 20 mg/dL and above compared with those whose levels were below 20. Among men with low HDL (less than 35 mg/dL) and high Lp(a), the risk was eight times higher.

One problem with interpreting Lp(a) values is that different ethnic populations vary widely in their normal ranges. Most experts don't recommend "treating" high Lp(a). However, when it occurs in people who have a very strong family history for heart disease but no other cholesterol problems, high total cholesterol, coronary artery disease, or damage to organs caused by high blood pressure, then it makes sense to intensify protective strategies, including diet, exercise, and drug therapy. Lifestyle changes don't

dose multivitamin. Though the group with the higher-dose multivitamin did lower their homocysteine levels more than the other group, both groups had an equal number of subsequent strokes and heart attacks. The results of this study should be interpreted with caution. It looked only at people who had already had a stroke, and it did not treat individuals because their homocysteine levels were high. So, it certainly does not prove that someone with heart disease who has a high homocysteine level would not benefit from lowering it.

More studies are under way to help determine that, but in the meantime, a reasonable recommendation is to do the things that are *thought* to lower homocysteine and *known* to promote a healthy heart, including taking a multivitamin and following the DASH diet. If it is proved that moderately elevated homocysteine levels don't cause heart disease, it's a good example of something that looks good at first but doesn't stand up to medical scrutiny. Bear this possibility in mind whenever you read about the "latest and greatest" in any medical field.

appear to lower Lp(a) levels, and neither do most medications. The one exception to this is high-dose niacin, which isn't always well tolerated by patients. Finally, for the majority of people, we just don't know whether lowering Lp(a) is beneficial.

Calcium

Since the early days of cardiac pathology in the late nineteenth century, doctors have known that calcium is deposited in the plaques of atherosclerosis, as it is anywhere in the body where inflammation occurs. Calcium puts the hardness in "hardening of the arteries."

So it seems logical that a test for calcium in the arteries would help diagnose heart disease. Until recently, we didn't have the technology to detect early buildups of calcium. After all, the coronary arteries are small, just 2 to 4 mm in diameter, and take many twists and turns as they travel around the heart muscle. And they are in constant motion, gyrating with each heartbeat. Think of trying to take a picture of a strand of spaghetti as it shimmies in boiling water, and you'll have some idea of what scientists face when they try to obtain images of the coronary arteries. It's a daunting task, but it is exactly what electron beam computed tomography (EBCT, also called ultrafast CT) has accomplished.

EBCT uses an electronically steered electron beam to produce x-rays. The beam can rotate around the patient much faster than an x-ray generator can, so EBCT is faster than other CTs—fast enough to take a picture of a beating heart. EBCT obtains each image in just $\frac{1}{20}$ of a second, about twenty times faster than a helical CT.

EBCT generates a calcium score that provides a very accurate measurement of the amount of calcium in a person's coronary arteries. The more calcium, the higher the score—and the more atherosclerosis.

But does the calcium score predict actual cardiac events? It does. Many studies have been completed to date, and most agree that people with the highest scores have the highest risk. A 2003 Illinois study of 8,855 people between the ages of thirty and seventy-six is a good example. None of the subjects had been diagnosed with coronary artery disease before their EBCTs. Each person provided information about his or her health and cardiac risk factors. The researchers tried to contact each subject after an average of thirty-seven months; they were able to reach 4,155 men and 1,484 women.

Although the men were younger (average age fifty) than the women (average age fifty-four), the men had higher average calcium scores (137 vs. 59). Even after taking standard cardiac risk factors into account, the 25 percent of men with the highest scores were four times more likely to suffer a heart attack or die from heart disease than the 25 percent of men with the lowest scores; they were also twenty-six times more likely to need bypass

If Calcium Is Bad for My Arteries, Should I Stop Eating It?

Dietary calcium has no effect on atherosclerosis. In fact, a moderate amount of calcium from non- and low-fat dairy products helps lower blood pressure, reducing cardiac risk.

operations or angioplasties. But although the calcium score did predict the need for surgery or angioplasty in women, it did not predict heart attacks or cardiac events.

This study is one of the most impressive demonstrations of the power of EBCT, but it has flaws. All the subjects referred themselves for scanning, so they may have had symptoms or other reasons to worry about their hearts. The scientists did not measure the cardiac risk factors themselves but relied on the subjects' own reports. Finally, the researchers were unable to contact more than a third of the original group. All these limitations make it hard to say that the results apply to the whole population of adults without cardiac symptoms. Still, experts agree that EBCT can detect coronary artery calcium and that high scores tend to indicate risk. However, an obvious weakness of EBCT is its inability to detect plaques that lack calcium (which includes many small plaques, the ones most likely to rupture and trigger heart attacks).

So should you run out and get an EBCT scan? Probably not, especially if you have a high or low risk for heart attack. The test is not likely to help low-risk individuals who would probably have low scores and are likely to stay healthy in any case. At the other extreme, high-risk individuals should receive treatment regardless of their calcium scores, so an EBCT is unlikely to help them. If your level of risk is in the middle, there might be a value in determining your calcium score to assess how aggressively to treat you, but as of now, it's unproved how valuable it would be. Plus, insurance companies most likely would not cover it. Like other high-tech diagnostic tests, EBCTs are now being marketed directly to the public. For a fee, you can bypass your doctor and buy yourself a scan. But should you? No. You and your doctor should work together to decide whether the test makes sense. Otherwise, you may just be wasting your money.

More research is needed to learn whether a high calcium score adds significantly to the information provided by much less expensive, better-studied risk indicators. And even if calcium scores add significantly to the risk profile, scientists will have to determine if this information leads to effective treatments and a better outcome. The large government Multi-Ethnic Study of Atherosclerosis is already under way, but it's not expected to answer these questions until around 2010. EBCT is an example of a recurring dilemma in modern medicine: technology has arrived before doctors have learned how best to use it.

Chlamydia Pneumoniae and Other Bacteria

What causes arterial inflammation in the first place? A possible contender is *Chlamydia pneumoniae*, a bacterium that can cause pneumonia, bronchitis, and sinus infections. *C. pneumoniae* routinely shows up in atherosclerotic plaques. In 2002, British researchers showed that five weeks of antibiotic therapy improved blood vessel function in people with angina who also had this bacterium in their blood.

The study doesn't prove that the microbes cause the plaques to build up. Indeed, the antibiotic might have been beneficial because it exerted an anti-inflammatory effect apart from its antibacterial action. Larger-scale antibiotic trials have not shown a reduction in heart attack rates. More research is needed, but if *C. pneumoniae* does pan out as an agent of inflammation, scientists may one day add antibiotics to their arsenal of standard treatments for coronary artery disease. Other bacteria, including the one that causes stomach ulcers, are also being studied for a link to heart disease.

Elevated Fibrinogen Levels

Fibrinogen is a blood protein that's critical to the clotting process and, as such, is essential to health. However, because in many cases blood clotting is the final event that blocks the coronary arteries, it's not surprising that studies have implicated elevated fibrinogen levels as a cardiac risk factor. Though fibrinogen levels can easily be tested, at present they aren't routinely measured because there's no known way to bring down high fibrinogen levels. It's also unclear whether reducing levels of fibrinogen would decrease the chance of getting heart disease or having a stroke. In some cases, however, regular exercise, weight loss, and quitting smoking can reduce elevated fibrinogen. Other interventions that prevent excessive blood clotting include taking low-dose aspirin or low-dose alcohol and eating a lot of fish.

An Unconventional Emerging Heart Risk Factor: Kidney Disease

Even mild kidney damage increases your chances of having a heart attack or stroke, or dying from one of these. And heart disease may be a warning sign that you have problems with your kidneys.

A big reason for this correlation is that both conditions often stem from the same sinister sources—high blood pressure, cholesterol-clogged arteries, inflammation, and high blood sugar. In a way, that's good news, because it means that treating heart disease often helps the kidneys, and vice versa.

If the heart is the body's engine, the fist-sized kidneys are part of its cleanup crew. They chemically filter the blood to remove waste products, toxins, and excess fluid. They regulate blood pressure and oversee the crucial balance of nutrients such as sodium, potassium, and calcium. And they make several vitamins and hormones.

Although the kidneys are tough, resilient workers, they aren't indestructible. Years of elevated blood pressure can damage them. Blood flow impeded by cholesterol-narrowed arteries causes problems in the kidneys, as do the high blood sugar and artery damage that accompany diabetes. In fact, the duo of high blood pressure and diabetes causes almost two-thirds of cases of kidney damage. Infection and inflammation account for most of the rest.

Kidney damage usually goes unnoticed until it's too late. By the time symptoms such as fatigue, poor appetite, weight loss, and itching appear, little healthy kidney remains. At this point, it may be necessary to start dialysis, essentially having a machine filter the blood three times a week.

Doctors use several yardsticks to measure kidney health. If you have heart disease, don't be surprised if your doctor asks you to get these tests. If he or she doesn't bring it up, you should.

- **Creatinine level.** Creatinine is a waste product that comes from the normal wear and tear of muscles. Healthy kidneys filter most of it out of the blood; weakened ones don't. So a simple blood test for creatinine offers a snapshot of your kidneys' health.
- **Glomerular filtration rate (GFR).** This measure—a calculation based on your creatinine level—estimates how well your kidneys remove wastes and fluids from your bloodstream. The higher the GFR, the better the filtration.
- **Protein level.** Most proteins in the bloodstream are too large to pass into the kidneys' millions of tiny filters (glomeruli). Damaged kidneys, though, let proteins pass into the urine. Checking the urine for protein, even at low levels, can serve as an early warning sign of kidney disease.

The following steps will help control damage to your kidney and heart.

- Control your blood pressure.
- Go easy on protein. There's some evidence that a high-protein diet can further weaken borderline or damaged kidneys by boosting blood pressure inside of them. If you eat a lot of protein, think about cutting back.
- Ask your doctor if you're on all the appropriate heart-protecting medicine. People who have both kidney disease and heart disease are less likely to get aspirin, beta-blockers, and statins than those who have just heart disease. Some

doctors worry that these drugs may further damage the kidneys. But a growing body of evidence indicates that the ability of these drugs to prevent heart attacks and strokes outweighs the possible negative effects they may have on the kidneys. However, this decision depends on a lot of individual factors, so talk with your kidney specialist.

- Check with your doctor before taking yellow-light drugs. Routine use of painkillers such as full-dose aspirin, ibuprofen, COX-2 inhibitors, and other nonsteroidal anti-inflammatory drugs can be hard on the kidneys. Acetaminophen is a good alternative.

How Heavily Should You Weigh Any Risk Factor?

With new risk factors seeming to emerge every day, it can be hard to know which ones to pay attention to. The search for new factors that influence heart disease is partly admirable scientific curiosity—a desire to know what goes wrong in heart disease and how to stop it. It also stems from a notion that has been bandied about in medical journals and textbooks without much proof—that about half of people with heart disease don't have any of the "traditional" risk factors. This means one or more of the big four: high blood pressure, high cholesterol, diabetes, or smoking.

In 2003, two teams of researchers decided to see whether the "only 50 percent" claim is true or whether it's the medical equivalent of an urban legend. One group looked at the medical records of almost four hundred thousand men and women who took part in three studies that followed the health and habits of these volunteers for twenty to thirty years to identify the causes of heart disease. The other group looked at records from more than one hundred thousand people with heart disease who volunteered for a dozen or so treatment trials.

In the treatment trials, a whopping 80 percent to 90 percent of the participants had at least one of the big four risk factors. In the follow-up studies, it was 90 percent to 100 percent. Keep in mind

Interpreting New Medical Information: Finding a Doctor Who Matches Your Style

The discussion of the role of emerging risk factors in clinical practice raises an important point about how the latest information in medical studies can be used to make health-care decisions. Many of the most important issues in medicine remain incompletely understood. Studies are published frequently that attempt to address those questions, but these studies often fall short of providing definitive answers. This is simply a reality and reflects the difficulty in performing experimental trials in humans.

The reasons a medical trial can produce a flawed or even incorrect answer are numerous. Sometimes a study has too few patients or it uses a population whose characteristics are completely different from those of the usual candidates for the diagnostic test or treatment. Sometimes a study is just poorly executed or has a serious design flaw that the investigators have failed to recognize. Despite these limitations, such studies can still be published, and their flawed or incomplete findings can make their way into the media or into a doctor's office.

Doctors have several choices when they read a study that is flawed or limited: they can ignore it; they can use the information in a very circumscribed way; or they can conclude that the study has really advanced the field and start employing the information broadly in their daily practice.

At academic medical centers like mine, we try to teach our medical students and other doctors in training to keep their practice of medicine based on well-performed, rigorous scientific studies. We try to teach them to recognize the essential features of a good study and the usual errors present in a poor one. The problem is that we all have to make decisions in our lives about situations for which we don't have all the information we need.

Medical decision making relies on clinical trials to point the way toward better choices, but we often have only incomplete or flawed studies to guide this decision-making process. Some doctors choose to be early adopters of information, and they practice at the leading edge of new findings. Others choose to wait until better evidence emerges. And, of course, there are plenty of doctors in between the two ends of this spectrum.

No one can flatly declare that one approach is better than another. The doctor who is an early adopter of medical information will occasionally bring a valuable new therapy to a patient, but he or she will also recommend practices that, in the end, prove to be of little or no value. In contrast, the later adopter will occasionally fail to bring a new advance to a patient in a timely manner, but that doctor is also much less likely to recommend therapies that are useless or even detrimental. Understanding where a doctor fits in this spectrum and picking one whose therapeutic temperament matches your own will go a long way toward making sure you get the kind of treatment you prefer.

Most doctors recognize this dilemma and are willing to have their decisions influenced by a patient's wishes. If you express a desire to have a more avant-garde diagnostic test or treatment, or a more conservative one, your doctor can incorporate that perspective into your treatment plan. Increasingly, medical insurance plans won't pay for tests or treatments that have not been proved to be valuable, but there are many exceptions to that rule. Having a conversation about this issue with your doctor can make a real difference in the care you receive whenever the science of medicine has yet to establish a clear approach.

that each of these studies worked backward, from heart disease to risk factor. The results *don't* mean that almost everyone with at least one of these factors will develop heart disease. But the results *do* make a strong case for paying attention to *all four* of the majors. Although the emphasis of this book is on cholesterol, the others deserve equal focus. If you have high blood pressure, high cholesterol, diabetes, a smoking habit, or any combination of these, focusing on them will help you live better and probably longer. Exercise, healthier eating habits, and getting to a healthy weight can do wonders for high blood pressure, high cholesterol, and diabetes. A variety of drugs can help get these under control and protect against their cardiovascular complications. And various approaches are helping more and more people stop smoking.

What about the newer factors like C-reactive protein or Lp(a)? They may add important information about your risk for heart disease, especially if you have a family history of heart trouble but an otherwise clean bill of health. For now, though, the biggest benefits will come from paying attention to the established risk factors.

CHAPTER 5

When You Visit Your Doctor

Most adults have probably had their total cholesterol measured, but as evidence continues to emerge about the different roles played by the different lipoproteins, we realize more and more how important it is to measure each lipoprotein separately. It's now recommended that everyone over age twenty should get a fasting lipid profile every five years. A fasting lipid profile measures your LDL, HDL, and triglyceride levels, not just your cholesterol level. Most of the time, you can get this test at your primary care doctor's office. As the name suggests, to prepare for the test, you need to fast. Avoiding alcohol for twenty-four hours and not eating for twelve hours before your appointment allow the doctor to get an accurate reading of your lipoproteins.

As explained in Chapter 1, triglyceride levels can fluctuate widely in some people depending on the food they eat, so it is a good idea to eat what you'd typically eat in the week or two before getting a lipid test. Triglyceride levels are also significantly elevated in the hours after eating a meal that contains any fat, which is why it is important to fast for twelve hours. Your LDL cholesterol level is almost always calculated using a formula that depends on the accurate measurement of a fasting triglyceride level, so if you couldn't resist that doughnut before your appointment, your triglyceride and LDL levels will be inaccurate.

The fasting is probably the most difficult part of the full cholesterol profile for most patients. Once you get to your doctor's office, someone will draw a tube's worth of blood and you're all done! Behind the scenes, the lab technician puts your blood into an automated chemical analyzer and runs the various lipid tests rapidly. If your triglyceride level is greater than 400, the lab can't calculate your LDL value. In more sophisticated labs, additional tests can be done to determine the LDL in that situation, but these require more costly and time-consuming procedures that are not always available. If that's the case, your doctor may send your blood to a national lab. LDL cholesterol can be measured directly by several different methods, each of which has its advantages and disadvantages, but all of which are more expensive than simply calculating LDL cholesterol from a standard lipid profile. So, if your LDL cholesterol can be determined by calculation, that is the preferred method and the one used in virtually all of the major cholesterol-lowering trials.

In addition to drawing your blood work, your doctor will perform a physical examination that can determine if you have other risk factors that will increase your likelihood of developing coronary disease. Typically, this involves measuring your blood pressure and checking your pulse to ensure that your heartbeat is regular and forceful. Sometimes your doctor will feel the thyroid gland in your neck to determine its size, as an under- or overactive thyroid can affect blood lipid levels. He or she may also feel the pulses of the carotid arteries in your neck and listen to blood flow through those arteries to ensure there are no blockages there. To assess your heart and cardiovascular function in more detail, most doctors will listen to your heart sounds and feel the pulses in your legs, which can be lost if there are significant blockages in any of the arteries that lead to the feet.

If your doctor finds anything abnormal, you generally will get further laboratory testing or imaging procedures. These could include an electrocardiogram (EKG), chest x-ray, echocardiogram (sound wave picture of the heart), or tests of thyroid or kidney function. Reduced pulses in the legs are often assessed by Doppler (sound wave) measurements or an equivalent noninvasive test. When these studies are completed and the lipid profile result has come back, your doctor is armed with the information needed to make recommendations about treating your lipid levels.

Inaccuracies in the Tests

Like most things in life, cholesterol measurements are not perfect. For one thing, in most labs, your LDL cholesterol is calculated based on the measurements of your total cholesterol, HDL, and triglyceride levels. As previously mentioned, if those levels are off, then your LDL measurement will be wrong as well.

A lot of things can affect a test's sensitivity and accuracy, including the method used to prepare the sample, the purity of the chemicals added to it, the skills of the technician, and the quality of the machine used to analyze the sample. A good lab can measure the same blood sample repeatedly and not have the total cholesterol level vary by more than about 3 percent.

Although the lab should not have more than a 3 percent variation in measuring your cholesterol level, your personal level may vary a good deal more when different blood samples are compared. One study showed that total cholesterol levels can fluctuate by as much as 11 percent over the course of a year. Researchers estimated that 60 percent of that variation was caused by biological fluctuations, and the remaining 40 percent by variations in the test itself. Changes in your average daily levels may reflect changes in your diet, smoking, illness, weight, exercise routine, or certain medications. That same study found that triglyceride measurements can vary anywhere from 12.9 percent to 40.8 percent, and HDL levels from 3.6 to 12.4 percent. This is why it's important to take more than one measurement if anything looks abnormal and not to overinterpret small changes in lipid values. If you see a small rise or fall in your levels from year to year, don't worry; it may not represent a real gain or loss.

Beyond HDL and LDL

Though HDL and LDL share the cholesterol spotlight, there are other lipoproteins floating around your bloodstream. Reading about them might help you better understand the effect of cholesterol in your body and on your health.

Chylomicrons

Chylomicrons (pronounced KYE-low-my-krons) have the highest ratio of fat to protein, and their job is to bring energy in the form of fat into muscles. Even though these molecules are high in fat, it's believed that they do not cause heart disease for two reasons. First, chylomicrons are 90 percent triglyceride by weight and have very little cholesterol in them. Second, people with normal lipid metabolism clear chylomicrons from the bloodstream about twelve hours after eating a fatty meal. In fact, this is the reason we ask patients to fast for twelve hours before getting a cholesterol test— so that chylomicrons will not be in the blood at all. This allows your doctor to get an accurate reading of the other lipoproteins, the ones that are thought to have more of an impact on heart disease risk.

If you have normal lipid metabolism, the intestines package the triglycerides from the fat in the food you eat into chylomicrons and

You can do some things to help control the biological variability part. First, try to have your blood drawn at the same time of day every time you have a test done, and follow a similar eating, exercising, and medication-taking pattern. Some other things can also help increase the accuracy, including avoiding alcohol for a few days before the test, sitting for at least five minutes before your blood is taken, staying seated during the procedure, and mentioning to your doctor any fevers you've had recently. As I already mentioned, if the results of one cholesterol test indicate that you need treatment, you should ask for another test a few

release them into the bloodstream. Chylomicrons then release many of their fatty acids into the body's tissues (like the heart and skeletal muscles), providing them with the energy they need to function. The rest of the chylomicron, the chylomicron remnant, travels on to the liver, where it is filtered out of the bloodstream.

The fatty acids carried in circulating chylomicrons may encounter one of three fates: they can be used for energy by various body tissues; they can be taken up by adipose (or fat) tissue and stored for future energy use; or they can go to the liver, where they are either used as fuel or resynthesized into triglycerides. If they go to the liver, that organ takes the resynthesized triglycerides, packages them with cholesterol and proteins, and releases the packages into the bloodstream as very low-density lipoproteins (VLDL).

Very Low-Density Lipoprotein (VLDL)
VLDL are made by the liver from fat, protein, and carbohydrates from your diet. They perform a similar function as chylomicrons—bringing fat to muscles so they can use it as energy. Unlike chylomicrons, however, when your body removes some triglycerides from a VLDL particle for energy, it becomes an LDL.

weeks later to verify the results so that you don't get put on a drug for life that you don't really need to take.

A Better Cholesterol Test?

About twenty years ago, people started to realize that measuring total cholesterol wasn't enough—you need to know your HDL and LDL breakdowns in order to best assess your risk. Along came the fasting full-lipid test. Now, some people are arguing that that isn't enough either. They say that measuring your LDL and HDL subfractions, along with other lipoproteins, gives you the best idea of which treatments are right for you. (Subfractions are basically just further breakdowns of the category of LDL or HDL, similar to how you could break down the category of low-fat milk into skim, 1 percent, and 2 percent.) A few companies offer these tests—namely Atherotec, Berkeley Heart Labs, and Liposcience. Though each uses a different method to get to the result, all of them generally measure the same things:

Direct LDL Measurement. In the basic lipid profile, LDL cholesterol is calculated by using a mathematical formula based on the measurements of triglyceride, total cholesterol, and HDL cholesterol levels. While this method has been widely used as the gold standard for determining LDL cholesterol levels for about forty years, it can be inaccurate under certain conditions. The higher the triglyceride level (especially above 250 mg/dL), the greater the potential error in calculation of the LDL value. According to some, this calculation can be off as much as 25 percent. And the worst part is that it underestimates the LDL level, making people think they have a healthier cholesterol level than they really do.

Newer tests measure the LDL cholesterol level directly, and they do not require that the blood sample come from a patient who has fasted for twelve hours. Although the accuracy and reproducibility of these tests have been more variable than I would like to see, they have been improved over the past few years and are widely used.

Measures for Different Types of LDL. Using these advanced tests, LDL gets broken down into two categories—one of which is smaller and denser than the other. Higher levels of the small, dense LDL are associated with higher rates of heart disease, partly because these smaller LDL can penetrate more easily into the lining of the arteries. A few large studies have found that high levels of small, dense LDL triple a person's risk for heart disease. Small, dense LDL particles also can't be reabsorbed by the liver as easily, which gives them more time to do their damage.

Measures for Different Types of HDL. Similarly, HDL can be sub-classified into denser and less dense particles. In this case, the different HDL particles are known as HDL 2 (less dense) and HDL 3 (more dense). Routine laboratory tests do not differentiate these two HDL particles—they just lump them together—but these more advanced tests do.

It is good to have high levels of both HDL 2 and HDL 3, but most studies indicate that high HDL 2 levels may be more potent in lowering your risk of heart disease than high HDL 3 levels. In a study of 1,799 Finnish men, for example, the risk of a heart attack was four times greater in men with low HDL 2 levels, three times greater in men with low HDL levels (not distinguishing HDL 2 from HDL 3), and only two times greater in men with low HDL 3 levels. Thus, it was low HDL 2 levels that carried the greatest risk. Stated another way, someone with particularly high HDL 2 levels would have the greatest protection.

Measures for Remnant Lipoproteins. Remnant lipoproteins (also called intermediate-density lipoproteins) are the particles that are trapped in between the conversion of triglyceride-rich VLDL to cholesterol-rich LDL. These particles are relatively rich in both triglyceride and cholesterol and can penetrate into the artery wall to stimulate atherosclerosis in much the same way that LDL particles do.

Measures for Lp(a). As discussed in Chapter 4, Lp(a) is an emerging risk factor for heart disease, and these new tests can measure for Lp(a) at the same time as measuring your other lipoprotein levels.

Should You Get a Specialized Cholesterol Test?

Knowing your specific lipid profile may allow you and your doctor to tailor your treatment accordingly. For example, if you have high small, dense LDL levels, your doctor may ask you to reduce your sugar intake, and if you have high triglyceride levels, you may need to reduce the sugar and alcohol in your diet. Your drug treatment may change depending on these tests as well. A statin or niacin may help with high remnant lipoproteins, for example, while niacin is the drug of choice for elevated Lp(a) levels.

However, for the most part, the specialized tests have not been convincingly demonstrated to improve upon the standard lipid profile in the prediction of coronary disease risk in the vast majority of patients. National guideline panels have not yet accepted these tests as better predictors of heart disease risk, and I do not yet routinely use these more expensive and complex lipid tests in my own practice. This is an area where advances in medical science could lead to changes in the testing we do in the next few years.

As they are substantially more costly than the standard lipid profile, I think that most patients should stick with the standard lipid tests for now. These are exceptions to this general rule:

1. People who have coronary disease but normal cholesterol levels as shown through a standard fasting test
2. People whose family members have a strikingly high rate of coronary disease despite a healthy lifestyle and a clean bill of health as reported by a fasting test

When to Treat Cholesterol

How do you and your doctor decide whether and how to treat your cholesterol? Even though high cholesterol is clearly linked to heart disease, you shouldn't make the decision about treatment based solely on your cholesterol numbers. I know, this sounds counterintuitive, but the point of treating high cholesterol is to prevent heart disease, and other risk factors besides cholesterol come into play when determining your risk of heart disease. So two people with the same cholesterol levels may walk out of their doctors' office with completely different advice: one may be told to fill a prescription for a cholesterol-lowering drug; the other may be told to get more exercise and eat better.

Things to Mention to Your Doctor if You Are About to Be Treated for an Abnormal Lipid Profile

Going to the doctor can be overwhelming or scary. And it's easy to forget to ask questions or mention recent events that might have skewed a blood test result. I suggest that you bring a written list of questions or topics you want to cover. Here are some issues you might want to bring up with your doctor when discussing your recent lipid profile:

1. Tell the doctor if you had a flu or other major or minor illness shortly before the blood test was performed. These events can dramatically alter the lipid profile, either reducing or elevating several of the lipoprotein fractions.
2. If your diet was dramatically different from your typical diet in the weeks leading up to the lipid test, this is worth noting, because high alcohol or carbohydrate intake can cause a dramatic elevation in serum triglycerides.
3. If you were expected to fast and didn't, don't be embarrassed to say so. You could end up on the wrong drug treatment if this error is not identified.
4. If there is an abnormality (i.e., high cholesterol levels when there hadn't been in the past), ask if your cholesterol will be measured again to make sure it wasn't a fluke.
5. Ask how you and your doctor will use the results to decide on a treatment plan.

Similarly, if you need treatment, its intensity should be based on your individual risk status. Preventing heart disease is definitely not a "one-size-fits-all" process—the higher your risk, the more aggressive your treatment, and vice versa. The National Cholesterol Education Program (NCEP) made this task of tailoring a treatment program to each individual's needs a little easier by publishing guidelines. These guidelines, updated most recently in

2004, base treatment on a person's risk factors and the likelihood that he or she will develop heart disease in the next ten years.

This next section of the book outlines the NCEP guidelines, which I and most other doctors use to make decisions about treatment. Your doctor may not go through each step with you explicitly, but ask him or her about the decision-making process and you're likely to hear something similar to what follows. You can also use the following information on your own to figure out your risk levels and what you can do to reduce your risk. But of course, you can't measure your lipid profile without help, and an overall assessment of the risks and benefits of drug treatment for anybody really requires a thoughtful conversation with a medical professional who can then prescribe the appropriate medications, if needed.

Step 1: Considering Your Cholesterol Levels

Once you have your cholesterol results back, you can compare them to what the NCEP guidelines consider to be favorable levels. (See Table 5.1.)

Total Cholesterol

Total cholesterol is the sum of cholesterol carried in all cholesterol-bearing particles in the blood including HDL, LDL, and VLDL. Although the total cholesterol level closely parallels the LDL level in most people, there are enough exceptions to that rule to make it useful to test for LDL, HDL, and triglycerides separately. The NCEP guidelines say a total cholesterol level of 200 mg/dL or below is desirable, 200–239 mg/dL is borderline-high, and 240 mg/dL is high.

HDL Cholesterol

HDL fights plaque buildup in the heart's arteries, and the more HDL you've got, the better. The NCEP guidelines consider levels of 60 mg/dL or above to be high enough to provide protection. HDL levels of less than 40 mg/dL are regarded as too low. Some clinicians use the ratio of total cholesterol to HDL choles-

TABLE 5.1 Categorizing Your Cholesterol and Triglyceride Levels

Total Cholesterol Level	Total Cholesterol Category
Less than 200 mg/dL	Desirable
200–239 mg/dL	Borderline-high
240 mg/dL and above	High

LDL Cholesterol Level	LDL Cholesterol Category
Less than 100 mg/dL*	Optimal
100–129 mg/dL	Near optimal/above optimal
130–159 mg/dL	Borderline-high
160–189 mg/dL	High
190 mg/dL and above	Very high

HDL Cholesterol Level	HDL Cholesterol Category
Less than 40 mg/dL	Low (representing risk)
60 mg/dL and above	High (heart-protective)

Trigylceride Level	Triglyceride Category
Less than 150 mg/dL	Normal
150–199 mg/dL	Borderline-high
200–499 mg/dL	High
500 mg/dL and above	Very high

*The 2004 update to the NCEP lists 70 mg/dL as an optional goal for patients with the highest heart risk to strive for.

Source: Adapted from National Institutes of Health, *Detection, Evaluation, and Treatment of High Blood Cholesterol in Adults (Adult Treatment Panel III)*, September 2002, page II-7.

terol to help identify people who need cholesterol-lowering therapy. The more HDL you have relative to total cholesterol, the smaller and healthier the ratio.

Reports from the Framingham Heart Study suggest that for men, a total cholesterol/HDL ratio of 5 means average risk, 3.4 means about half the average risk, and 9.6 means double the average risk. For women, a ratio of 4.4 works out to be average risk, 3.3 is half the average, and 7 is twice the average.

For the vast majority of people, the difference between using the HDL level and the ratio of total cholesterol to HDL doesn't much matter. Most people with a high level of total cholesterol also have an unfavorable ratio and would be targeted for intervention under either system. Still, a few people may find that the ratio provides a strikingly different assessment of their coronary risk. Someone with a desirable total cholesterol of 195 mg/dL—who would be labeled low risk under the old system—might in fact be headed for heart disease if his or her total cholesterol/HDL cholesterol ratio was too high due to a low HDL level. Conversely, someone with a cholesterol level of 250 mg/dL—who would ordinarily be put on a treatment program—might actually need little more than the usual lifestyle changes if a high HDL level (and thus a low ratio) accounted for a good proportion of the total.

LDL Cholesterol

Your LDL levels are the most significant of the blood lipids in terms of raising your risk for heart disease, so lowering your LDL should be the primary target of therapy. For LDL cholesterol, below 100 mg/dL is optimal, 100–129 mg/dL is near optimal/above optimal, 130–159 mg/dL is borderline-high, 160–189 mg/dL is high, and 190 or above is very high. The July 2004 NCEP update states that an LDL level as low as 70 is an option for people at the highest risk. The panel also noted that if you need to go on cholesterol-lowering medication, it makes sense for most people to aim for a 30 percent to 40 percent reduction in LDL cholesterol, not a smaller reduction that gets you to a particular LDL level. So if you and your doctor determine your LDL goal should be 100 mg/dL, and your LDL level is currently at 115 mg/dL, it doesn't make sense to take a low dose of medicine that gets you to the 100 mg/dL mark. Instead, you should probably take a higher dose that gets you down to 80 mg/dL or so. Depending on your other cholesterol levels and other risk factors, your therapy to lower LDL may involve lifestyle changes, such as diet and exercise, or the use of cholesterol-lowering medication.

Triglycerides

Many studies have indicated that as the triglyceride level rises, so does heart disease risk, but the link seems to vary depending on what other risk factors are present. Triglyceride levels also vary considerably in response to what a person has eaten just before the blood test. And many substances or medical conditions can cause high triglyceride levels, including uncontrolled diabetes, corticosteroids or thiazide diuretics, or too much alcohol.

The NCEP guidelines recommend aggressive treatment for elevated triglycerides. Recent studies indicate that an elevated triglyceride level is significantly linked to the degree of heart disease risk. The 2001 guidelines recommend treating even borderline-high triglyceride levels. Therapy includes weight control and physical activity—and sometimes, for higher triglyceride levels, medication.

The guidelines for triglyceride levels say that below 150 mg/dL is normal, 150–199 mg/dL is borderline-high, 200–499 mg/dL is high, and 500 mg/dL and above is very high. High triglyceride levels should prompt a search for an underlying cause, such as alcohol abuse, liver disease, medications, an underactive thyroid gland, or undetected diabetes. People with combined hyperlipidemia, a condition marked by high LDL and high triglyceride levels, often suffer from a genetic disorder, although some of them have acquired the condition as the result of being obese or using alcohol heavily.

Step 2: Determining if You Have Heart Disease or Diabetes

People who have heart disease have a much greater chance of having a heart attack than those who don't. In fact, more than twenty out of every one hundred people with heart disease will have recurrent heart disease within ten years. Heart disease, for the purpose of estimating this risk, is broadly defined and includes coronary artery disease as well as diseases of the arteries outside of the heart. Atherosclerosis in the arteries outside of the heart is generally called peripheral artery disease and can include blockages or enlargements (aneurysms) that affect the neck (carotid), abdominal (aortic), or leg arteries. Symptoms of peripheral arterial disease depend on the site of the blockage, but they can include sudden loss of vision; pain in the calf, thigh, or buttocks when walking; or impotence.

We now know that diabetes carries similar risks for heart health. So if you have any of the previously mentioned heart conditions, especially in combination with diabetes, you'll probably be in the most aggressive treatment group (very high risk), so you can skip over the next few steps that help determine that category and go to Step 6. If you have diabetes but are very young and free from heart disease or other risk factors, you might not need such aggressive treatment. If you fall into that category, you will most likely be in the high-risk category; skip to Step 6.

If you don't have a heart problem or diabetes, go to Step 3.

Step 3: Measuring Your Risk Factors

As discussed in Chapter 4, there are a lot of risk factors that increase your chance of having a heart attack. Count your major risk factors, which include these:

- Cigarette smoking
- High blood pressure (greater than 140/90 mm Hg or treated with a blood pressure medication)
- Family history of early heart disease (at younger than fifty-five in male first-degree relatives and sixty-five in female first-degree relatives)
- Aged over forty-five in men and fifty-five in women

Although the other risk factors noted in Chapter 4 are not included in this part of the analysis, you and your doctor should take their presence or absence into consideration.

If you have one or fewer of the major risk factors, skip to Step 5. If you have more than one, go on to Step 4.

Step 4: Calculating Your Heart Attack Risk

The worksheet in Figure 5.1 (pages 98–99), based on the NCEP guidelines, will help people who have two or more major risk factors determine their risk of having a heart attack in the next ten years. You can use it to add up your points and then determine your risk level. Note that a 3 percent risk means that three out of one hundred people with your risk profile will have a coronary event in the next ten years, a 10 percent risk means that ten out of one hundred people with your risk profile will have a coronary event in the next ten years, and so on. Also note that there are separate heart attack calculators for men and women.

Step 5: Finding Your Treatment Category

Armed with your responses from Steps 1 through 4, use the following information to figure out which treatment category you fit into.* In addition, you can determine what your LDL goal should be.

Very High Risk

You are considered at very high risk if you have established cardiovascular disease AND one or more of the following:

- Multiple major risk factors for cardiovascular disease, especially diabetes
- Severe and poorly controlled risk factors, especially smoking
- Multiple risk factors for metabolic syndrome, especially high triglycerides (200 or above) and low HDL (below 40)
- A history of recent heart attack or unstable angina

Your LDL Goal. Below 70 mg/dL. This is an optimal goal that your physician may recommend if you are in this category.

---

* Adapted from National Institutes of Health, *Detection, Evaluation, and Treatment of High Blood Cholesterol in Adults (Adult Treatment Panel III)*, September 2002, and Scott M. Grundy, et al., 2004, "Implication of Recent Clinical Trial for the National Cholesterol Education Program Adult Treatment Panel III Guidelines," *Circulation*, 110:227-239.

FIGURE 5.1 Heart Attack Calculator for Men

Heart attack calculator for men
(To calculate your risk for developing heart disease in the next ten years)

I. Age

Age	Points
20–34	–9
35–39	–4
40–44	0
45–49	3
50–54	6
55–59	8
60–64	10
65–69	11
70–74	12
75–79	13
Score: _____	

II. Total cholesterol level (mg/dL)   Score: ___

Age	20–39	40–49	50–59	60–69	70–79
<160	0	0	0	0	0
160–199	4	3	2	1	0
200–239	7	5	3	1	0
240–279	9	6	4	2	1
≥280	11	8	5	3	1

III. Do you smoke?   Score: _____

Age	20–39	40–49	50–59	60–69	70–79
Nonsmoker	0	0	0	0	0
Smoker	8	5	3	1	1

IV. HDL level   Score: ___

HDL (mg/dL)	Points
≥60	–1
50–59	0
40–49	1
<40	2

V. Blood pressure (mm Hg)   Score:___

Systolic	Untreated	Treated
<120	0	0
120–129	0	1
130–139	1	2
140–159	1	2
≥160	2	3

Total points: I. ____ + II. ____ + III. ____ + IV. ____ + V. ____ = _____

Scoring

Your ten-year heart attack risk by points

Points	≤0–4	5–6	7	8	9	10	11	12	13	14	15	16	≥17
% Risk	≤1	2	3	4	5	6	8	10	12	16	20	25	≥30

Adapted from National Institutes of Health, Detection, Evaluation, and Treatment of High Blood Cholesterol in Adults (Adult Treatment Panel III), September 2002, pages III-4–III-5. For an online version go to nhlbi.nih.gov.

FIGURE 5.1 Heart Attack Calculator for Women

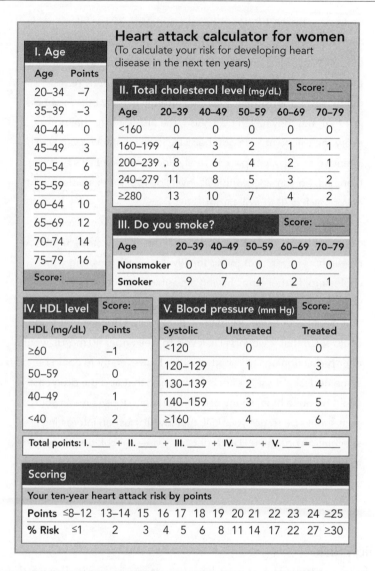

Heart attack calculator for women
(To calculate your risk for developing heart disease in the next ten years)

I. Age

Age	Points
20–34	–7
35–39	–3
40–44	0
45–49	3
50–54	6
55–59	8
60–64	10
65–69	12
70–74	14
75–79	16

Score: _____

II. Total cholesterol level (mg/dL)   Score: _____

Age	20–39	40–49	50–59	60–69	70–79
<160	0	0	0	0	0
160–199	4	3	2	1	1
200–239	8	6	4	2	1
240–279	11	8	5	3	2
≥280	13	10	7	4	2

III. Do you smoke?   Score: _____

Age	20–39	40–49	50–59	60–69	70–79
Nonsmoker	0	0	0	0	0
Smoker	9	7	4	2	1

IV. HDL level   Score: _____

HDL (mg/dL)	Points
≥60	–1
50–59	0
40–49	1
<40	2

V. Blood pressure (mm Hg)   Score: _____

Systolic	Untreated	Treated
<120	0	0
120–129	1	3
130–139	2	4
140–159	3	5
≥160	4	6

Total points: I. _____ + II. _____ + III. _____ + IV. _____ + V. _____ = _____

Scoring

Your ten-year heart attack risk by points

Points	≤8–12	13–14	15	16	17	18	19	20	21	22	23	24	≥25
% Risk	≤1	2	3	4	5	6	8	11	14	17	22	27	≥30

Adapted from National Institutes of Health, Detection, Evaluation, and Treatment of High Blood Cholesterol in Adults (Adult Treatment Panel III), *September 2002, pages III-4–III-5. For an online version go to nhlbi.nih.gov.*

How Low Will They Go?

Right now, the NCEP doesn't suggest making 70 mg/dL a goal for everyone—only those at the highest risk level. Why? Well, first, though the studies on which the new update is based are strong, they are not conclusive enough to warrant completely new guidelines. Other studies that are currently in the works might do just that, but they haven't yet. Also, the NCEP notes that not everyone will be able to get their LDL levels that low. Even with intensive therapy, people can rarely decrease their LDLs by more than half. So someone with LDL levels of 150, for example, might never reach a 70 mg/dL target.

As the recommendations for LDL cholesterol keep creeping downward, you might be wondering if they'll ever stop. Right now, researchers haven't yet found the level at which lowering your cholesterol further stops having a positive impact on health. So while the new optional goal is 70 mg/dL, future studies may find that even lower levels are helpful. Personally, I believe that studies could show that lowering LDL levels to well under 40 mg/dL would offer protection against heart disease. However, there could be some undesirable side effects from doing that and the drug cost could be quite high, so my opinion certainly doesn't mean your goal should be to get your LDL that low. It's just an interesting speculation on where LDL targets may go—speculation that needs to be backed by clinical studies before anyone adopts that goal.

High Risk

You are at high risk if you have a history of heart disease (heart attack, unstable or stable angina, a heart procedure such as angioplasty or bypass) OR the "risk equivalent" of having had heart disease AND a ten-year risk of more than 20 percent of having a heart attack. The risk equivalent includes having diabetes or evidence of diseased blood vessels (peripheral artery disease, blocked carotid arteries, transient ischemic attacks, etc.) along with two or more risk factors for heart disease (cigarette smoking, high blood pressure, a family history of premature heart disease).

Your LDL Goal. Less than 100 mg/dL. Drug therapy is recommended if you have not been able to lower your LDL to this level with diet and exercise changes.

Moderately High Risk

You are considered to be at moderately high risk if you have two or more risk factors for heart disease (cigarette smoking, high blood pressure, a family history of premature heart disease, age) and a 10 percent to 20 percent chance of having heart disease in the next ten years.

Your LDL Goal. Less than 130 mg/dL. Begin with diet and exercise changes. Your doctor may recommend lowering your LDL to less than 100 mg/dL with medication.

Moderate Risk

Having two or more risk factors for heart disease and a less than 10 percent chance of having heart disease in the next ten years puts you at moderate risk.

Your LDL Goal. Less than 130 mg/dL. Begin with diet and exercise changes if your LDL is 130 mg/dL or above, but consider drug therapy at LDL levels of 160 mg/dL or above.

Low Risk

You are at low risk if you have one or no risk factors for heart disease.

Your LDL Goal. Less than 160 mg/dL. Begin with diet and exercise changes if your LDL is 160 mg/dL or above, but consider drug therapy at an LDL level of 190 mg/dL or above.

Step 6: Determining Your Treatment

Based on the previous information, you are able to determine three things:

- The LDL level you should strive for
- The LDL level that should compel you to change your lifestyle
- The LDL level at which you should consider going on drug therapy

I'll go over how to achieve these goals in depth in the next chapters, but here are some general drug and lifestyle recommendations based on your category.

Very High Risk

In 2004, the NCEP issued guidelines that made 70 mg/dL an optional goal for people at the highest risk of heart disease. This is 30 mg/dL lower than the previous goal for this group of people. Why the change? In recent years, new studies have indicated the benefit of lowering cholesterol to levels well below 100. These studies found that for every 1 percent decline in LDL cholesterol, risk for a heart event declines by 1 percent—and that this relationship applies to cholesterol levels even below 100 mg/dL. Some people think that as more studies on the benefits of low cholesterol come out, LDL goals will continue to fall.

The committee notes that the 70 mg/dL target should be only for people in the highest risk category, meaning those with heart disease and one of the characteristics listed on page 97. If you fall into this high-risk category and have high uncontrolled cholesterol levels, you and your doctor can decide what combination of drug and lifestyle therapy is right for you. If you belong in this category but have an LDL cholesterol level at or near 70 mg/dL, either with or without cholesterol-lowering medication, there are a few options, depending on individual characteristics. You and your doctor should decide whether you should take any of the following actions:

- Start or intensify lifestyle or drug therapies to specifically lower LDL cholesterol
- Delay such treatment in favor of first trying to change other risk factors or in favor of trying drugs to increase HDL cholesterol or decrease triglycerides
- Lose weight and increase activity if you have metabolic syndrome (see "What Is Metabolic Syndrome?")

What Is Metabolic Syndrome?

A person with metabolic syndrome has three or more of the following:

- A large waist (forty inches or more for men and thirty-four inches or more for women; to measure your waist size, don't go by your belt measurement—instead, wrap a tape measure around the largest part of your midsection and make sure you keep the tape measure parallel to the floor)
- Borderline or high blood pressure (anything above 130/85 mm Hg)
- A high level of triglycerides (above 150 mg/dL)
- Low HDL (under 40 mg/dL for men or 50 mg/dL for women)
- High fasting blood sugar (above 100 mg/dL)

What does metabolic syndrome do to the body? Doctors and researchers think that metabolic syndrome's impact on health is more than the sum of its parts. Basically, in people with this disorder, blood sugar levels stay high after a meal or snack instead

(continued)

103

What Is Metabolic Syndrome?, *continued*

of dropping to a base level as they do in most people. The pancreas, sensing still-elevated glucose levels, continues to pump out insulin. Constant high levels of insulin and blood sugar have been linked with many harmful changes, including damage to the lining of coronary and other arteries, increased triglyceride levels in the blood, changes in how the kidneys handle salt, and blood that clots more easily. Chronic overstimulation of the pancreas may exhaust it so that it stops supplying enough insulin.

This cascade of changes isn't healthy. Damage to artery walls, high triglycerides, and increased chance of blood clots can lead to heart attacks and some strokes. Changes in the kidneys' ability to remove salt contribute to high blood pressure, another path to heart disease and stroke. And dwindling insulin production by the pancreas signals the start of type 2 diabetes, which greatly increases the chances of having a heart attack or stroke, as well as nerve, eye, and kidney damage.

Even after heart disease appears, the metabolic syndrome continues to complicate things. Among almost sixty-five hundred men and women who had bypass surgery, for example, those with metabolic syndrome were four times more likely to have died within eight years of their surgery than those without it. This syndrome was especially hazardous for women, who were thirteen times more likely to have died.

Researchers from the Centers for Disease Control and Prevention applied the given definition of metabolic syndrome to almost nine thousand people who took part in the Third National Health and Nutrition Examination Survey. In this sample, about 23 percent had the metabolic syndrome. Applied to the entire United States, this would mean about forty-seven million Americans have this problem. The treatments outlined in the next chapters can decrease the chance that you'll have the symptoms that characterize metabolic syndrome.

High Risk

If you fall into this category and have an LDL cholesterol level above 100, you should do all that you can to control other risk factors through lifestyle changes. However, you're probably going to need a cholesterol-lowering drug to get your cholesterol levels into the safe zone, so you should probably also start on medicine.

Moderately High Risk

The 2004 NCEP guidelines separate the moderate-risk group into two. Some people in this group should use an LDL goal of 130 mg/dL while others should aim for 100 mg/dL. How do you know which is for you? Your doctor might ask you to adopt the lower goal if you are older or have any of the following:

- More than two risk factors or severe risk factors (like continuing to smoke cigarettes or a strong family history of early heart disease)
- Triglycerides above 200 mg/dL combined with total cholesterol minus HDL cholesterol that is above 160 mg/dL
- HDL cholesterol below 40 mg/dL
- Metabolic syndrome

For everyone else in this group, if your ten-year risk is 10 percent to 20 percent and your LDL level is 130 or higher, you should start with lifestyle changes. If in three months your LDL levels haven't decreased, you may want to start on an LDL-lowering drug.

If your ten-year risk is 10 percent or less, you should start with lifestyle changes, and as long as your LDL is reduced to 160 or lower, continue without medication. If your LDL is higher than 160, medication may be necessary.

Moderate Risk

You should try to keep your LDL levels under 160 by having a healthy lifestyle. If your cholesterol is higher than that despite

Treatment to Get Your LDL Very Low and Its Side Effects

In one of the recent studies that caused the NCEP to issue an update to its cholesterol guidelines, a high-dose statin (80 mg) was needed to get LDL levels below 100 mg/dL. Though the people in the study tolerated the high dose well, the chance of having a side effect increases with dose, so if you are put on a high-dose statin, you and your doctor should be extra vigilant about watching for side effects, especially muscle pain that might signal a muscle-wasting disorder.

Previous epidemiological studies have suggested a link between very low cholesterol and an increase in death rate, but some researchers think this finding might be due to factors other than the low cholesterol level. New studies have not found any significant side effects linked to very low LDL levels.

lifestyle changes, you may want to try drug therapy, particularly if you have any of the following:

- One risk factor that's severe, such as very low HDL cholesterol or a heavy smoking habit
- Multiple nonmajor or emerging risk factors
- A ten-year risk approaching 10 percent or LDL levels of 160 or higher

Low Risk

You (and everyone, really) should follow the lifestyle recommendations outlined in Chapters 6 and 7 to keep your heart-disease risk at this healthy level.

Personalizing the NCEP Guidelines

Guidelines are not rules for everyone. If you and your doctor note that you have a lot of secondary risk factors that the NCEP guidelines don't take into account, you may decide to treat your high cholesterol more aggressively than the NCEP guidelines indicate. Or if you have a lot of lifestyle risk factors that you are willing and able to change, maybe you and your doctor will want to assess your cholesterol levels again after a few months of your new habits before you try a cholesterol-lowering drug.

It's also important to keep in mind that the NCEP guidelines exist in a bit of a vacuum. They're updated every few years to include major breakthroughs, but in the years between updates, the already-published guidelines can't take into account studies that come out. And of course, a doctor's experience with an individual patient or a subgroup of patients may tell him or her that there's a better way to handle your case.

CHAPTER 6

A Diet to Lower Your Cholesterol

If the last chapter (or a discussion with your doctor) made you realize that you need to lower your cholesterol, this chapter and the next two chapters will tell you how. I'll discuss lifestyle changes first, then medications. I like to do so in this order for two reasons. One, some people might need to just change their habits to get their cholesterol levels in check. Two, even people who do need medication should also adopt these lifestyle changes. This will not only help lower your cholesterol further but will also give you many other benefits.

Benefits of Adopting a Heart-Healthy Lifestyle

There's no doubt that lowering the amount of LDL cholesterol sliding through your bloodstream can reduce your odds of having a heart attack. Data from dozens of studies indicate that the chance of being stricken with a heart attack drops 20 percent to 30 percent with effective LDL lowering. If you're someone with unhealthy eating habits (think cheeseburgers and fries) and you switch to a diet low in saturated fats, you can decrease your cholesterol by 25 percent or more! That said, the average person will see a drop of 5 percent to 10 percent on a moderately low-fat diet and 15 percent on a severely restricted diet. These are still very beneficial changes. Although lowering your cholesterol will not guarantee you protection from heart attack or stroke, it can substantially improve your odds.

Your Cholesterol-Lowering Diet

Many people have been on a host of different diets in their lives. Maybe you've tried Weight Watchers, the Zone, or, more recently, the Atkins diet. While any of those plans can help you lose weight, they're not the philosophy I ask my patients to adopt. I tell them to think of a diet not as something that's going to restrict specific foods but as a new attitude toward eating. Instead of thinking of eating as something you do to satisfy cravings that are going to come back the more you satiate them, I tell patients to think of food as the very thing that keeps their body going. Put healthy foods in, you'll get a healthy life out.

I'll first go over some food facts to keep in mind, and then I'll outline strategies that can help you adopt and stick with this healthy eating regimen.

The Truth About Fat

Until recently, fat and health were as compatible as oil and water. A prerequisite for making your diet healthier was to cut fat down to no more than 30 percent of your daily calories—the less the better. More than 30 percent, many nutrition experts said, would set the stage for heart disease, obesity, cancer, and other ills. Several major health organizations endorsed this view, and the big fat scare was on. Cookbook authors, diet programs, and the media all jumped on the low-fat bandwagon. The alternative view, held for decades by many leaders in nutrition research, was that the key to health was the *type*, not the amount, of fat.

The second view turned out to be correct. Fat is a major energy source for your body and also helps you absorb certain vitamins and nutrients. In the average American diet, about 35 percent of calories come from fat. People trying to reduce their cholesterol level should try to keep their fat intake between 25 percent and 35 percent of their calories.

But just as important as the amount of fat you eat is the type. Saturated fats (found mainly in meat, butter, whole milk, and cheese) and trans fats (which come mostly from the partially hydrogenated oils used in restaurant fryers, many margarines, and packaged snacks and baked goods, and in lesser amounts from dairy products and meats) are the ones to stay away from. Saturated fats increase heart attack risk by increasing LDL cholesterol and triglycerides. Trans fats do the same, but they also pack a second punch: they actually decrease the heart-healthy HDL cholesterol levels. Good fats, on the other hand, decrease your LDL cholesterol. That's why indiscriminately cutting fat out of your diet isn't a good idea—it could actually worsen your cholesterol profile.

Good fats include monounsaturated fats and omega-3 and omega-6 polyunsaturated fats. The polyunsaturated fats are the healthiest, which is why so many dietary recommendations include fish.

The NCEP guidelines say that only 7 percent of your daily calories should come from saturated fat. Unfortunately for lovers of red meat, butter, ice cream, and cheese, these foods are rich in saturated fats and their intake should be carefully rationed. It is not possible to avoid saturated fat entirely because even the healthiest oils are mixtures of saturated and unsaturated fats.

And contrary to previous expert advice, holding your fat intake to the low end of the spectrum is not necessarily healthier than letting it reach 35 percent. A low-fat diet is no guarantee of good health. In fact, a diet with only 20 percent of calories from fat can be virtually a junk-food diet if you make up for the lost fat calories with sugary foods such as soft drinks, nonfat cookies, and high-starch carbohydrates such as white bread and potatoes. An overabundance of these foods increases the risk of heart disease and diabetes.

What's the difference between a good fat and a bad fat? All fats have a similar chemical structure: a chain of carbon atoms bonded to hydrogen atoms. What differs is the length of the chain and the shape of the carbon atoms in the bonds they form with each other and the hydrogens. Seemingly slight differences in structure translate into crucial differences in the way the body handles these fats.

Bad Fats. The two forms of unhealthy fat, saturated and trans fats, share a physical trait: they are solid at room temperature. Think of butter or the marbleized fat in a steak. But not all the foods that contain a lot of bad fats are solid. Whole milk, ice cream, and some oils also contain abundant amounts of bad fats.

- **Saturated fats.** The word *saturated* refers to the number of hydrogen atoms these fats have. In a saturated fat, the chain of carbon atoms holds as many hydrogen atoms as possible, making it literally saturated with hydrogen atoms. Each carbon atom in the chain is connected to the next by a single bond, leaving the maximum number of bonding points available to hold hydrogen.

  There are about twenty-four different saturated fats. Not all of them are equally bad for your health. The saturated fat found in butter, whole milk, and other dairy products increases LDL levels the most, followed by the saturated fat in beef. Curiously, the saturated fat called stearic acid, found in pure chocolate, is more like unsaturated fat in that it lowers LDL levels. Even some vegetable oils such as palm oil and coconut oil contain saturated fat.

- **Trans fats (partially hydrogenated oils).** These fats occur naturally in meat, but their main source is packaged baked products such as cookies, cakes, breads, and crackers, as well as fast foods and some dairy products. Trans fats were artificially created in the laboratory about a hundred years ago to provide cheap alternatives to butter. Food chemists found that they could solidify vegetable oil by heating it in the presence of hydrogen. The process, called hydrogenation, gives the carbon atoms more hydrogen atoms to hold. As a result, the structure of polyunsaturated fat (a good fat) becomes more like saturated fat. Thus, solid vegetable fats such as shortening and margarine came into being. Today, trans fats are found not only in solid foods such as these but also in foods that contain "partially hydrogenated oil." Even some cooking oils are partially hydrogenated to keep them fresh.

The Institute of Medicine expert panel says that trans fats have no known health benefits and that there is no safe level. In 2006, food manufacturers will be required to list the amount of trans fats a product has. Until then, the words *hydrogenated* or *partially hydrogenated* in the ingredients list are the red flags. Keep purchases of oils and packaged foods with these words in their ingredients to a minimum, and try to find products with the lowest amount of these substances whenever possible.

Good Fats. Good fats come mainly from vegetable and fish products. They differ from bad fats by having fewer hydrogen atoms bonded to their carbon chains. They are liquid, not solid. There are two broad categories of beneficial fats: polyunsaturated and monounsaturated.

- **Polyunsaturated fats.** When you pour liquid cooking oil in a pan, there's a good chance you're using polyunsaturated fat. Corn oil is a common example. Polyunsaturated fat has two or more double carbon bonds. There are two major types of polyunsaturated fats: omega-3 (n-3) fatty acids and omega-6 (n-6) fatty acids. (The numbers refer to the distance between the end of a carbon chain and the first double bond.) Polyunsaturated fats are essential fats, meaning they are vital to normal body functions, but your body can't manufacture them. Therefore, it's important to get polyunsaturated fats from food. Polyunsaturated fats help build cell membranes, the exterior casing of each cell,

If Fish Is Good for Me, Should I Take a Fish Oil Supplement?

Interest in the heart-healthy benefits of fish oil dates back about two decades, beginning with a 1980 study showing that Eskimos in Greenland—who eat nearly a pound of fish a day—have low rates of mortality from heart disease. In subsequent years, there has been substantial research on the effects of fish oil on the heart and arteries. Laboratory studies have shown that fish oil, which contains what are known as n-3 or omega-3 fatty acids, makes blood platelets less sticky, helps protect the linings of arteries, and may also lower blood pressure.

Population studies from several countries have shown lower rates of heart disease in people who eat fish regularly. In 1998, data from the Physicians' Health Study showed that eating fish once a week versus less than once monthly halved the likelihood of dying suddenly from a heart attack. Total heart attack rates (including heart attacks that led to nonsudden death) and total cardiovascular deaths were not affected by fish consumption or the amount of omega-3 fatty acids ingested. One year later, a report in the *Lancet* described a randomized trial in which men who'd had a heart attack received either a fish oil supplement, 300 mg of vitamin E, both, or neither. The group who received the fish oil supplement had significantly lower rates of heart attack, stroke, or death during the next three and a half years. Sudden-death rates dropped by 45 percent.

Additional support for fish oils comes from a report on nearly eighty thousand women in the Nurses' Health Study. Published in

and the sheaths surrounding nerves. They're vital to blood clotting, muscle contraction and relaxation, and inflammation. They reduce LDL cholesterol more than they lower HDL, improving your cholesterol profile. Even better, they also lower triglycerides.

2001 in the *Journal of the American Medical Association,* this fourteen-year study found that eating fish at least twice a week versus less than once a month cut in half the risk of strokes caused by clots blocking an artery to the brain. The Nurses' Health Study also found that eating one to three servings of fish per month cut the risk of heart disease by 20 percent, while eating at least five servings a week lowered risk by 40 percent.

Anyone hoping to benefit from fish oil would probably be better off sticking with dietary sources, primarily from cold-water fish such as salmon, trout, mackerel, sardines, and herring. Forgoing meat for cold-water fish—or any fish for that matter—may lower cholesterol and heart disease risk simply by reducing the amount of saturated fats in your diet.

Three groups of people may benefit from fish oil supplements. One group includes people with arrhythmias, or disordered heart rhythms. The omega-3 fatty acids in fish oil can stabilize wayward electrical activity in the heart and calm arrhythmias. The second group includes people with high levels of triglycerides, especially those who can't control the problem through diet and exercise, because fish oil supplements have been shown to help lower triglycerides. The third group includes people with coronary heart disease. The American Heart Association recommends that these people eat one serving of fatty fish a day; recognizing that this may be more fish than most people will eat, the association notes that a supplement can be substituted.

Both the omega-3 fatty acids and omega-6 fatty acids offer health benefits. Research has shown that omega-3s help prevent and even treat heart disease and stroke. Evidence also suggests they have similar benefits against autoimmune diseases such as lupus, eczema, and rheumatoid

How to Avoid Trans Fats

In principle, it should be easy to avoid synthetic trans fats. After all, humans did without them (except the small amount found in meat) until the early 1900s. But now it's more complicated because packaged and convenience foods—especially cookies, cakes, crackers, chips, and other snacks—are ubiquitous and usually loaded with trans fats. Trans fats are also found in many restaurant and fast foods, certain cereals, and even some energy and nutrition bars.

Since the updated trans fat labeling is strictly voluntary until 2006, how do we know what foods to avoid now? If we stop eating margarine, fried foods such as doughnuts and French fries, and certain prepared foods, we'll cut out at least half the trans fats available in the American diet.

Here are some additional strategies for lowering your intake of trans fats:

- Be label savvy. If a product lists shortening or partially hydrogenated or hydrogenated oil as one of its first ingredients, it has a lot of trans fat. Avoid it, or eat it only in very small quantities.
- If you're eating out, beware of foods fried in partially hydrogenated oils. Some fast-food establishments list nutrition information on wall posters or make it available in a handout.

arthritis. Omega-3s come mainly from fish but also from flaxseeds, walnuts, canola oil, and unhydrogenated soybean oil. Fatty fish such as salmon, tuna, mackerel, and sardines are especially good sources of omega-3s. The Institute of Medicine has set the daily reference intake (DRI) for alpha-linolenic acid, the omega-3 in vegetable oils, at 1.6 grams per day for men and 1.1 for women.

Omega-6 fatty acids also lower the risk for heart disease. High levels of linoleic acid, an omega-6, are in such

- Do some math. Some labels include enough information to allow you to figure out trans fat content, even if it's not listed. If the grams of polyunsaturated fat and monounsaturated fat are given, add them to the grams of saturated fat and subtract the sum from "total fat." What's left is trans fat.

- Choose the better spreader. Generally, the softer a margarine is at room temperature, the better—that is, the lower in trans fat. One that's labeled trans fat–free is your best bet. Or try using olive oil on your bread or cooked vegetables. If you must choose between butter and a margarine whose trans fat "credentials" are not clearly marked, go with the butter—products that are free of trans fat usually feature that fact prominently on the label, and gram for gram, trans fats are worse than the saturated fats in butter.

- Fry and sauté wisely. Use canola oil or olive oil. And be on the lookout for true-but-tricky advertising in restaurants and on packages of frozen fried foods. Food that's fried in partially hydrogenated vegetable oils is often labeled "cholesterol free" and "cooked in vegetable oil."

- Make it yourself. Trans fats are also found in unexpected places—commercial breads, soups, cereals, bean and other dips, and packaged entrées. Whenever possible, make these foods from scratch, using nonhydrogenated fats.

vegetable oils as safflower, soybean, sunflower, walnut, and corn oils. The DRI for linoleic acid is 17 grams per day for men ages nineteen to fifty and 12 grams for women that age. For adults ages fifty-one to seventy, the DRI is 14 for men and 11 for women.

- **Monounsaturated fats.** When you swab your bread in olive oil at an Italian restaurant, you're getting mostly monounsaturated fat. Unlike a polyunsaturated fat, which has two or more double bonds of carbon atoms, a monounsaturated fat has just one. The result is that it has more hydrogen atoms than a polyunsaturated fat but fewer than a saturated fat. Although there is no DRI for monounsaturated fats, the Institute of Medicine recommends using them as much as possible along with polyunsaturated fats to replace the bad saturated fats and trans fats. Good sources of monounsaturated fats are olive oil, peanut oil, canola oil, avocados, and most nuts.

The Right Carbohydrates

Just like fat, there are good and bad carbohydrates. Though your choice of carbohydrates doesn't have a major impact on your LDL cholesterol level, it can affect your triglyceride and HDL cholesterol levels substantially.

Carbohydrates encompass a broad range of foods, including table sugar, fruits and vegetables, and grains such as rice and wheat. The DRI for carbohydrates is 45 percent to 65 percent of your daily calories. But, as the Healthy Eating Pyramid (Figure 6.1) shows, most of these carbohydrates should come from whole-grain foods, vegetables, and fruits. If most of the carbohydrates you eat are bad carbohydrates (white bread, potatoes, white rice, and other white starches at the top of the Healthy Eating Pyramid), you could end up gaining weight and putting yourself at risk for some serious diseases.

A 2002 report in the *Journal of the American Medical Association* cited several dozen studies that have found that people who eat a lot of starchy foods are at higher risk for obesity, heart disease, and diabetes compared with people who eat such foods in moderation. A study in the *Journal of the National Cancer Institute* in 2002 found that women who were overweight and sedentary and who ate a lot of starchy foods were two and a half times as likely as other women to get pancreatic cancer.

The list of bad carbohydrates may come as a surprise. Why are potatoes bad for you? They're vegetables, after all. Why are they in the same category as sweets? To answer these questions, you have to consider the glycemic load, a measure of how quickly a

FIGURE 6.1 The Healthy Eating Pyramid

Adapted with permission from Walter C. Willett, M.D., Harvard School of Public Health.

serving of food is converted to blood sugar during digestion and how high the spike in blood sugar is. In general, the good carbohydrates have a lower glycemic load than the bad carbohydrates (see Table 6.1). The glycemic load of your diet can significantly affect your risk for diabetes, heart disease, and possibly obesity.

TABLE 6.1 Glycemic Load: High or Low?

High Glycemic Load Foods	Low Glycemic Load Foods
Crackers	Barley
French fries	Bran
Honey	Brown rice
Potatoes	Bulgur wheat
White bread	Lentils
White rice	Oatmeal
Refined cereals	Whole fruits
Soft drinks	Whole-grain cereals
Sugar	

The Atkins Diet and Cholesterol

In the past few years, the Atkins diet and other low-carbohydrate diets have boomed in popularity. As more and more people adopted the low-carbohydrate, high-protein, high-fat diet, food manufacturers and restaurants began promoting products to fit into this eating plan. Some of the low-carb diets (like the South Beach diet) distinguish between good fats and bad fats, but some (like Atkins) don't. Without any advice on which fats to eat, people tend to load up on the bad ones that they love: bacon, cheese, steak, and fried foods, for example. But this approach leads to an unbalanced diet that's way too high in saturated fats.

In fact, a study that used various equations to estimate the impact of certain diets on long-term health estimated that the Atkins diet would raise the average American's cholesterol by 51 mg/dL. However, in more surprising news, some recent studies found that low-carb diets have a similar effect on cholesterol levels as low-fat diets, or in some cases even a better effect. For example, a six-month study of seventy-nine obese people found that the low-carb diet had a similar effect as a low-fat diet on HDL and LDL levels, but a more favorable impact on triglyceride levels.

But other studies have found the opposite. So at this point there's just not enough unbiased information out there to give a green light to eating bacon cheeseburgers (with or without the bun) every day. Plus, with what we do know about diet and cholesterol, it is illogical to conclude that long-term consumption of a low-carb, high–saturated fat, high-protein diet would be heart-healthy:

- The link between saturated fat and heart disease is well established, and studies also suggest an increased risk for stroke, but that link is not as strong.
- Low-carb diets are very low in fiber. Many studies worldwide link a high intake of fiber with a reduced risk of heart disease and diabetes.

(continued)

The Atkins Diet and Cholesterol, *continued*

- The Atkins diet is very low in fruits and vegetables. Many studies link a high intake of fruits and vegetables with a reduced risk of heart disease and stroke.
- Low-carb diets are very high in protein. Protein is essential for health, and in animals, large amounts of protein accelerate the aging of the kidneys, and high-protein diets are harmful for some people with kidney disease. But there is no evidence in healthy humans that large amounts are harmful. In addition, a high intake of protein causes calcium loss that may increase the risk of osteoporosis and kidney stones.
- These diets are likely to be high in sodium (salt). A high intake of sodium is associated with an increased risk of high blood pressure in some people.
- The best study to date on the subject found that even though low-carb dieters lose weight faster than low-fat dieters, at the end of a year, the two dieters are neck and neck in the weight-loss race.
- Low-carb diets often do lower trigylceride levels nicely, and they may have a less pronounced effect on lowering HDL, which often happens on low-fat diets. So, if you have high triglycerides, a low-carb diet could lead to a substantial reduction in triglycerides and also total cholesterol, though it is unlikely to have a beneficial impact on LDL cholesterol.

Foods with a high glycemic load are digested more quickly than foods with a low glycemic load. Rapidly digested foods can be a problem because they flood your bloodstream with a lot of sugar all at once. Sudden, high spikes of blood sugar trigger a gush of insulin to clear the sugar from your blood. The problem is that this quick surge of insulin can leave your blood sugar too low after just a few hours. When your blood sugar is too low, you feel hungry; if it's low soon after a meal, you're apt to overeat and possibly gain weight.

Another problem with a steady diet of meals high in glycemic load is that over many years, your body's system of responding to insulin could be impaired. This is called insulin resistance. When your cells are less responsive to insulin, the resulting overload of sugar in your bloodstream forces the pancreas to step up its production of insulin in an effort to move the sugar from the blood into the cells. If the pancreas is forced into overdrive for a sustained period, it may wear down and eventually stop producing insulin altogether, leading to insulin deficiency and type 2 diabetes—the more common type of diabetes, which typically develops in late adulthood. Insulin resistance can also cause other problems, including unhealthy cholesterol profiles, heart disease, and perhaps some cancers.

Choosing Good Carbohydrates. The high–carbohydrate foods that are good for you can help protect against these health problems in part because they have a relatively low glycemic load. They are digested slowly, which means they cause a gradual rise in blood sugar. Building your meals and snacks around foods with a low glycemic load appears to have many health benefits. It may help you maintain a normal weight and protect you against heart disease, diabetes, and some forms of cancer. As a rule, carbohydrates have higher glycemic loads than do proteins and fats. But the good carbohydrates, such as legumes, nuts, and whole grains, usually have lower glycemic loads than the bad, starchy carbohydrates, such as potatoes.

You can estimate whether a carbohydrate is good or bad based on these characteristics:

- **How swollen is the starch?** The more a starchy food absorbs water and expands when cooked, the faster it is digested and the higher its glycemic load. White rice expands more than brown rice does. Potatoes (white potatoes, russets, red potatoes, and others in this family) expand more than do sweet potatoes (which are not related to white-fleshed potatoes, despite their name). Pasta has a somewhat lower glycemic load because it is digested more slowly, especially if it is cooked al dente rather than overcooked until it is swollen and soft.

- **How heavily processed is the food?** One factor in a grain product's glycemic load is its degree of refinement. In general, the smaller the pieces, the faster they are digested. This is one reason finely ground wheat flour is digested faster than coarsely ground (sometimes called "stone-ground") wheat flour. Some scientists think that the glycemic load of the average American diet has increased in recent years because we're eating greater amounts of heavily processed carbohydrates. Processing removes the fibrous casing from grains. This casing is good for you because it slows digestion and contains a host of nutrients that may lower the risk of some diseases. Studies show that whole-grain foods such as brown rice and barley, which have their fibrous casing intact, are healthier than the more heavily processed refined grains. In two large ongoing studies, the Nurses' Health Study and the Health Professionals Follow-Up Study, people who ate the most whole grains (about a bowl of oatmeal and two slices of whole-wheat bread daily) were less likely than other people to develop type 2 diabetes, heart disease, and several types of cancer, including cancer of the mouth, stomach, colon, gallbladder, and ovary.
- **What proportion of the food is whole-grain?** Not all foods in the grocery store that seem to be "whole-grain" really are. "Whole-wheat" bread may include refined, white flour. Look for labels that say "100 percent whole wheat" (or oats or rye). Read the ingredients list to make sure that the first ingredient is a whole grain. Some whole-grain foods can be easily spotted by their color. Brown rice is a whole grain (it's brown because its casing is intact), but white rice isn't.

123

Boosting Your Fiber Intake

You can probably identify some high-fiber foods, such as bran cereals and whole-grain breads. But not all foods billed as "high fiber" really have much fiber; read the labels on packaged foods to see the number of grams of fiber they contain. You can be sure of getting fiber if you eat fruits, vegetables, and whole-grain foods such as whole-wheat bread, brown rice, and oats each day. The amount of fiber that you should get (also known as fiber's *dietary reference intake*, or DRI) varies with age and gender. Men fifty and under should get 38 grams per day, while women that age should get 25 grams per day. Older men and women should aim for 30 and 21 grams per day, respectively. Here are some ways to make sure that your diet meets the DRI for fiber:

- **Eat whole-grain cereal for breakfast.** Oatmeal is an excellent choice. Steel-cut oats have the most fiber. If you prefer cold cereal, choose products that have bran or list whole wheat, oats, barley, or another whole grain first on the list of ingredients.
- **Choose whole-grain breads.** As with cereals, true whole-grain breads list a whole grain first in the ingredients. Whole-grain sliced bread, pita, and rolls are equally good.
- **Skip the French fries and baked potatoes.** Instead of white potatoes, eat sweet potatoes or yams. Instead of white rice, eat brown rice or another intact grain as a side dish. Good choices are kasha, bulgur, millet, quinoa, and barley.

- **How much fiber is in the food?** Fiber is the indigestible part of grains, vegetables, and fruits. Its effect is to delay the time it takes for the food to be digested, and some kinds of fiber can lower cholesterol. Whole–grain foods have more fiber than refined foods.
- **How much fat is in a meal or snack?** Because fats take longer to digest than carbohydrates, the more fat a meal or

- **Try whole-wheat pizza and pasta.** Prepared pizzas made with whole-wheat crust are joining whole-wheat pastas on supermarket shelves. Try pasta dishes that mix whole-wheat pasta with white pasta.
- **Cook with whole-wheat flour.** You can make pancakes, muffins, and home-baked goods healthier if you mix whole-wheat flour with white flour. Because whole-wheat flour is heavier than white flour, a straight substitution won't work for every recipe. Try starting with a ratio of one part whole wheat to three parts white to see if you like the results. If you think the dish could stand a heavier, grainier texture, try increasing the share of whole-wheat flour. You may need to increase the amount of liquid at the same time.
- **Take fiber supplements.** Fiber can also be taken in the form of supplements, which provide the same benefits as fiber in foods. Take them with plenty of water to get the full benefit.

Fiber's sterling reputation was slightly tarnished by findings that it doesn't prevent colon polyps, precursors of colon cancer. Also, it reduces LDL cholesterol only slightly. But it is still considered one of the most important health attributes of foods. Beware that increasing your fiber intake can cause flatulence, particularly if you go straight from eating little fiber to eating a lot. Slowly increasing the amount of fiber in your diet can help.

snack has, the more slowly it will be digested and, possibly, the less detrimental an effect it will have on your blood sugar. Just make sure that the fat is one of the good fats. Pasta with olive oil and roasted vegetables is far healthier than a burger and fries. A handful of cashews or other nuts is a better snack than a cookie made with butter or trans fats.

TABLE 6.2 Cholesterol Levels in Some Common Foods

Food	Serving Size	Cholesterol (mg) per Serving
Scrambled egg	1 large	214
Fried chicken	½ breast	119
French toast with butter	2 slices	116
Beef, top sirloin, fat trimmed to ¼", cooked	3 oz	76
Tuna sub	1 6" sandwich	48
Hamburger	1 sandwich	29
Chocolate cake with chocolate frosting	1 piece	26
Beef and pork frankfurter	1 frank	22
Cheese pizza	1 slice	9

Source: USDA National Nutrient Database for Standard Reference

What About Dietary Cholesterol?

I saved talking about dietary cholesterol levels to last because it's fairly obvious: if you want to decrease your cholesterol levels, you should ingest less cholesterol! The NCEP guidelines recommend less than 200 mg of dietary cholesterol per day. For reference, one large egg yolk has 200 mg. See Table 6.2 for the amount of cholesterol in some other foods.

The Diet-Cholesterol Connection

For some people—let's call them responders—blood cholesterol levels rise and fall pretty directly in relation to the amount of cholesterol and fat in their diets. In others, there's little connection. The same goes for dietary fat. A 1997 study done at the Human Nutrition Research Center on Aging at Tufts University looked at how 120 men and women responded to the same low-fat, low-cholesterol diet recommended by the NCEP. On average, LDL levels dropped. Yet though everyone ate the same thing—the researchers provided the volunteers with all their food and drink—the average result masked a wide range of LDL responses, ranging from a 55 percent decrease to a 3 percent *increase* among men and a 39 percent decrease to a 13 percent *increase* among women. Because there isn't a simple way to test whether you're a

True-but-Tricky Package Labels

Surprisingly, the effect of eating cholesterol-rich foods on raising your blood cholesterol level is less than the effect of eating foods high in saturated fat. The food industry has often labeled products in ways that are technically correct but, in my opinion, medically misleading. A food that is low in cholesterol content but rich in saturated fat is worse for your blood cholesterol than one that is higher in cholesterol but lower in saturated fat. The take-home lesson here is read the label on low-cholesterol foods carefully to make sure that the saturated and trans fat contents are not high.

responder before you try an improved diet, the only way to gauge this is to limit dietary fat and cholesterol and see what happens. If your cholesterol doesn't drop, you can still stick with the healthier food choices, but at a minimum you will know whether your diet is playing an important role in your elevated cholesterol level.

Finding the Diet That's Right for You

The Tufts University study brings up an important fact about dieting in general and cholesterol lowering in particular: everyone is different! A diet that helped your friend lose weight and lower her cholesterol might not work for you, because of either biological or lifestyle differences. What you need to do is find a plan that works for you and stick with it. Don't get discouraged if you have to try a few different kinds before one feels right.

One trick that works for some people is keeping a food diary. For some reason, knowing that they have to write down that trans-fat-loaded brownie or high-fat hamburger makes them think twice before biting down. It's also a good way to see what your eating habits are in black and white—they may turn out to be different from what you think!

If you're a very social person, it might help you to call in some "diet reinforcements" in the form of friends. If they're looking to eat healthier, too, you can talk about or e-mail each other your daily diet diary. Hearing "Good job!" or "You'll do better tomorrow" can go a long way toward helping you stick with your plan. Other systems, like rewarding yourself with a small (nonedible!) treat each day or week that you do well may also provide motivation. Again, what works for you depends on who you are as a person, so try some different methods and see what feels right.

Remember, too, that if you slip one day or week and fall back into your old eating patterns, you shouldn't give up. Old habits can be stubborn. Don't be too hard on yourself; just start over again as many times as you need to. Eventually, your new habits will become your norm.

Monitoring Your Progress

Figuring out whether your diet is working can be hard. First of all, most people want to see results immediately, and when the pounds don't start flying away within the first week, they convince themselves the diet isn't working. On a healthy diet, you can expect to lose only about one to two pounds a week.

Another good way to monitor your progress is to get your lipid profile checked after about two or three months of your new diet, and then again at six months. If you're a "responder," you should see a drop in your LDL cholesterol. Once you have reached your target levels, have a follow-up every six months to make sure your cholesterol is staying at a healthy level. Depending on your cholesterol levels, if you don't see a drop in LDL cholesterol, you may need to either see a dietitian for a more thorough review of food choices and diet plans, or start on drug therapy.

CHAPTER 7

An Exercise Program to Lower Your Cholesterol

Some of my patients complain that they just hate to exercise. What I say to them is that they just haven't found the activity that's right for them. And just like eating healthy, exercising is a habit that you have to form. On top of that, being inactive is a habit you have to break. But once you make exercise a consistent part of your life, you'll miss it when you don't do it—you'll miss the feeling of doing something healthy for yourself, the occasional soreness of your muscles that reminds you that you're getting healthier, and the overall sense of well-being that exercise brings on.

The Benefits and Risks of Exercise

Exercise's impact on heart health is amazing. Research has shown that even moderate exercise can substantially reduce the incidence of coronary events. Aerobic exercise reduces cardiac risk by lowering triglycerides and raising HDL cholesterol levels; by reducing blood pressure, body fat, blood sugar, and mental stress; and by moderating the blood's propensity to clot.

Exercise also improves the heart's pumping ability, which greatly enhances the body's functional capacity and stamina. And it's never too late to start. Healthy people who begin exercising after age forty-five can reduce their death rate by 23 percent over the next twenty years or so, and even patients who've already had heart attacks can use medically supervised aerobic exercise to reduce their risk for another heart attack by up to 25 percent.

Sedentary living, on the other hand, is the fifth major cardiac risk factor. Because it increases the risk for coronary artery disease by almost two times, a lack of exercise is nearly as dangerous as smoking, abnormal cholesterol levels, or hypertension.

What kind of exercise is best? If you're usually sedentary, the most important thing is to incorporate almost any kind of physical activity into your daily life. Gardening, housework, and even taking the stairs count as light exercise. More regular, sustained exercise is even better. Your goal is to eventually incorporate the three main types of exercise into your week: aerobic exercise, strength training, and stretching.

Aerobic exercise, which employs large muscle groups in a rhythmic, repetitive fashion for prolonged periods of time, has long been considered the best type of exercise for the heart. Examples include brisk walking, jogging and running, biking, swimming, aerobic dance, rowing, cross-country skiing, and brisk singles racket sports.

All patients with heart disease should discuss any exercise program with their doctor BEFORE they begin. Along with personal advice, he or she will tell you to not do any activity that causes chest pain (angina) or that exceeds the activity threshold documented on your stress test.

Regular exercise does raise your risk for minor injuries, such as shin splints or sprains and strains. But if you talk to your doctor before you start a program, choose a low-impact activity, take it slowly at first, and very gradually increase the intensity of your program, the benefits—lower total cholesterol, lower triglycerides, higher HDL, lower blood pressure, better control of blood sugar, a stronger heart that pumps blood more efficiently, even a better mood—far outweigh the risks.

A Program to Get You Started

An exercise program doesn't just happen on its own. It takes thought and perseverance to develop a routine that's tailored to your needs. Your first priority should be finding an activity and a schedule that you can stick with over the long haul. To give yourself the best chance for success, start out gradually, set realistic goals, and reward yourself for accomplishments along the way.

This section includes sample programs for each of the three main fitness components: aerobic activity, strength training, and flexibility exercises. For the aerobic components, I focus on walking because it's an activity that almost everyone can do safely—even people with a heart condition—and it's inexpensive. If you're more inclined to biking or swimming, just substitute those activities. You can mix and match parts of these sample programs to create a personal fitness routine, or you can fold these activities into an existing routine. Of course, check with your doctor before starting this or any exercise program to make sure it's appropriate for you.

Core Aerobic Program

In the past, walking may have had the unfair reputation of not being "real" exercise. After all, most people do it every day without a second thought. But times have changed, and walking has gained new respect.

Before you take your first steps, follow these guidelines to plan your program:

- **Find a safe place to walk.** Options include quiet streets, trails in parks, athletic tracks at local schools, or a shopping mall.
- **Invest in a good pair of shoes.** Shoes for walking should have thick, flexible soles that cushion your feet and elevate your heel a half to three-quarters of an inch above the sole. The upper portion of the shoe should be constructed of "breathable" materials such as nylon mesh or leather.

- **Consider choosing a partner or a group to walk with.** Having company helps some people stay motivated. Depending on where and when you walk, it can also ensure your safety. However, if you use your exercise time as an opportunity for reflection, solitude may be more appealing.
- **Wear clothes appropriate to the season.** Wear lighter clothes than you'd need if you were standing still; you'll warm up as you exercise. Dress in layers so you can peel off garments if you get hot.
- **Stretch before you walk.** (The ten basic stretches outlined later in this chapter can get you started.)
- **Warm up and cool down.** Include five-minute warm-up and cooldown segments as part of your total walking time.
- **Practice good walking technique:**
  Walk at a brisk, steady pace. Slow down if you're too breathless to carry on a conversation.
  Hold your head up, and lift your chest and shoulders.
  Keep your back straight, and gently contract your stomach muscles.
  Point your toes straight ahead.
  Let your arms swing loosely at your sides. If you want to boost your speed, bend your elbows at a 90-degree angle and swing your hands from waist to chest height.
  Land on your heel and roll forward onto the ball of your foot, pushing off from your toes. Walking flat-footed or only on the ball of the foot may lead to soreness and fatigue.
  Take long, easy strides, but don't strain. To go faster, take quick steps instead of long ones.
  Lean forward slightly when walking fast or up or down hills.
- **Create a walking program that works for you.** Use Figure 7.1 to get started.

FIGURE 7.1 Sample Walking Program

	Sessions per Week	Warm-Up	Walking Time	Cooldown	Total Minutes
Week 1	2	5 min. slow walking	5 min. brisk walking	5 min. slow walking	15 min.
Week 2	3	5 min. slow walking	5 min. brisk walking	5 min. slow walking	15 min.
Week 3	4	5 min. slow walking	10 min. brisk walking	5 min. slow walking	20 min.
Week 4	5	5 min. slow walking	10 min. brisk walking	5 min. slow walking	20 min.
Week 5	6	5 min. slow walking	10 min. brisk walking	5 min. slow walking	20 min.
Weeks 6–7	6	5 min. slow walking	15 min. brisk walking	5 min. slow walking	25 min.
Week 8	6	5 min. slow walking	20 min. brisk walking	5 min. slow walking	30 min.
Week 9	6	5 min. slow walking	25 min. brisk walking	5 min. slow walking	35 min.
Week 10	6	5 min. slow walking	30 min. brisk walking	5 min. slow walking	40 min.
Week 11	6	5 min. slow walking	40 min. brisk walking	5 min. slow walking	50 min.
Week 12	7	5 min. slow walking	50 min. brisk walking	5 min. slow walking	60 min.

Step-by-Step

Because humans don't come equipped with built-in speedometers, you need some way to measure your walking speed. The easiest way is to count your steps per minute. Provided you're walking on level ground, you can use the following values to gauge your pace:

Slow = 80 steps per minute

Brisk = 100 steps per minute

Fast = 120 steps per minute

Racewalking = More than 120 steps per minute

Follow the plan in Figure 7.1 to build up your strength and endurance. If you haven't been exercising, start at the beginning. If you're already exercising but want to increase your activity, start at the level that best matches your current routine and build from there.

Flexibility: Ten Basic Stretches

Stretching exercises that increase flexibility are another key component of fitness. When done regularly, the following simple stretches can help you to stay limber, avoid injury, and improve your balance and posture. Unless otherwise indicated, repeat each of the following stretches three to five times.

Hamstring Stretch

Stretches: Back of thigh

How it's done: Sit sideways on a bench without leaning back. Keep your shoulders and back straight. Keep one leg stretched out on the bench, straight. Keep your other leg off the bench with your foot flat on the floor. Lean forward slowly from the hips (not the waist) until you feel a stretch behind the knee and in the calf of the leg on the bench. Hold that position for ten to thirty seconds. Repeat three to five times with each leg.

Calf Stretch

Stretches: Lower leg muscles

How it's done: Stand in front of a wall with your arms outstretched, your hands on the wall, and your elbows straight. Step back one to two feet with one leg, placing it so your heel and foot are flat on the floor. Hold this position for ten to thirty seconds. Then, bend the knee of the stepped-back leg, keeping your heel and foot flat on the floor. Hold the position for ten to thirty seconds. Repeat three to five times with each leg.

Triceps Stretch

Stretches: Back of upper arm

How it's done: Bend your right arm behind your neck, pointing your elbow toward the ceiling. Grasp your elbow with your left hand, gently putting pressure on the raised right elbow until you feel a mild stretching at the back of your upper right arm. Hold the position for ten to thirty seconds. Repeat on the other side.

Shoulder Stretch

Stretches: Shoulders and upper back

How it's done: Sit comfortably on the edge of a chair. Raise your arms. Lace your fingers together and extend your arms upward, with palms toward the ceiling. Keep your shoulders drawn back behind the line of your ears, and keep your eyes straight ahead. Hold for ten to thirty seconds.

Quadriceps Stretch

Stretches: Front of thighs

How it's done: Lie on your side on the floor. Raise your head with your hand or a pillow. Your hips should be aligned one on top of the other. Bend the knee that is on top, and grab the heel of that leg. Pull until the front of your thigh feels stretched. Hold for ten to thirty seconds. Reverse position and repeat with the other leg.

Side Stretch

Stretches: Trunk, side, and shoulder muscles

How it's done: Sit up straight in a chair. With your left hand resting
lightly on your left leg, reach upward as far as you can with your
right hand. You should feel a stretch along your rib cage, trunk,
and waist. Hold for ten to thirty seconds. Reverse sides and
repeat.

Double Hip Rotation

Stretches: Outer muscles of hips and thighs

How it's done: Lie on your back with your knees bent and your feet
flat on the floor. Keep your shoulders on the floor at all times.
Keeping your knees together, gently lower your legs to one
side. Hold the position for ten to thirty seconds. Bring your
knees back to the center and repeat on the other side.

Single Hip Rotation

Stretches: Muscles of pelvis and inner thigh

How it's done: Lie on your back on the floor and bend your knees.
Let one knee slowly lower to the side. Hold the position for ten
to thirty seconds. Bring that knee up to center, keeping your
shoulders flat on the floor throughout the exercise. Repeat with
the other knee.

Neck Rotation

Stretches: Neck muscles

How it's done: Lie on your back on the floor with a telephone book
or some other thick book supporting your head. Slowly turn
your head from side to side, holding the position for ten to
thirty seconds on each side.

Lower-Back Stretch

Stretches: Muscles of the lower back

How it's done: Lie flat on your back with both legs extended. Bend
one knee and clasp it with both hands, pulling it toward your

chest as far as it will comfortably go. Breathe in deeply and exhale, bringing the knee closer as you breathe out. Hold the position for ten to thirty seconds, continuing to breathe. Repeat with the other leg.

Strength Training

Though strength training's role in heart health is less developed than aerobic exercise, it can be a rewarding addition to your aerobic routine. Here are some basic strength-training tips:

- Aim for two to three twenty-minute strength-training sessions a week.
- Don't perform strength training on the same muscle groups on consecutive days.
- Work all your major muscle groups: arms, shoulders, legs, and torso.
- Start with a weight that's comfortable but challenging. If you're just beginning, start conservatively and increase the weight by increments as needed rather than risk straining a muscle or injuring yourself. If you can't comfortably do eight repetitions of an exercise, your weight is too heavy. If you can do more than fifteen repetitions, it's too light.
- Move only the part of your body that you're trying to exercise. Don't rock or sway.
- Lift the weight slowly. Take three seconds to lift, hold the position for one second, and take another three seconds to lower the weight again.
- Breathe slowly, exhaling as you lift and inhaling as you lower the weight.
- Never hold your breath.
- Do one set of eight to fifteen repetitions of an exercise, rest for thirty to sixty seconds, and then do another set. As you gain strength, you may want to add a third set.
- Include a warm-up period before you start your strength-training program, and cool down when you finish.

How Much Should You Exercise?

In 1996, the Surgeon General recommended exercising enough to burn at least 150 calories—the equivalent of walking about one and a half miles per day. But in the beginning, this might be unrealistic. Start with an amount you're comfortable with—even ten minutes of walking a day—and work your way up as that becomes easier and easier. As physical activity becomes a more regular and enjoyable part of your routine, try gradually working up to thirty to forty-five minutes of brisk walking or its equivalent per day. (Table 7.1 will give you an idea of the number of calories burned during different activities.)

Aerobic exercise should be stimulating but not stressful; it should take effort but not be exhausting. Once you're reasonably fit, you should be able to sustain it for twenty to thirty minutes or longer. Another good way to measure your intensity is that if you can't talk while you do it, you're probably going too hard; if you can sing while you do it, you're probably not going hard enough. Remember to do a five- to ten-minute warm-up and cooldown before and after each session of aerobic activity to avoid injury. Doing the same activity you have planned at a lower intensity (walking slowly before a power walk, for example) is a great way to accomplish this.

Fitting Exercise into Your Life

You may be wondering how you're going to fit these new activities into your already busy life. I can't tell you how to get more hours in a day, but I can tell you that exercise is too important not to find time for it. If you want to exercise for half an hour a day, think about substituting it for something you now do for thirty minutes. Do you really need to watch two hours of television in the evening? Could the thirty minutes you spend sending e-mails to friends during lunch be shortened? Could you convince your neighbor to join you so you can socialize and exercise at the same time? Be realistic. Don't schedule exercise for after dinner if you

TABLE 7.1 Calories Burned During Thirty Minutes of Activity

Activity	125 lb. Person	155 lb. Person	185 lb. Person
Weight lifting (general)	90	112	133
Stretching, hatha yoga	120	149	178
Aerobics (low impact)	165	205	244
Aerobics (high impact)	210	260	311
Stair-climbing machine (general)	180	223	266
Stationary bicycling (moderate)	210	260	311
Elliptical trainer (general)	270	335	400
Walking: 3.5 mph (17 min/mile)	120	149	178
Bowling	90	112	133
Dancing: slow, waltz, fox-trot	90	112	133
Dancing: disco, ballroom, square	165	205	244
Golf (using cart)	105	130	155
Golf (carrying clubs)	165	205	244
Swimming (general)	180	223	266
Walk/jog: jog <10 min	180	223	266
Tennis (general)	210	260	311
Basketball (playing a game)	240	298	355
Bicycling: 12–13.9 mph	240	298	355
Running: 5 mph (12 min/mile)	240	298	355
Gardening (general)	135	167	200
Mowing lawn (push power mower)	135	167	200
Shoveling snow (by hand)	180	223	266

know that's when you always have to help the kids with their homework.

In addition to the time you schedule every day, look for ways to add bits of activity and recreational exercise—an extra lap around the mall when you're shopping or a Saturday morning bike ride, for example. Studies show that you can get some cardiovascular benefits even if you break up your thirty minutes of daily exercise into three or four eight- to ten-minute sessions, as long as they are of moderate intensity. However, it's unsafe to do frequent bouts of high-intensity activity.

After the first week, adjust your schedule in places where it may not be working. The good news is that as your conditioning increases, you'll be able to boost the intensity of your exercise without further exerting yourself. This means that you'll be able to fit more into your allotted time; for example, you'll be able to walk four miles in the time it used to take you to do three.

Designing the Right Program

It should come as no surprise that the most successful exercise program is one well suited to the individual. To give yourself the best odds of sticking with a program, stack the deck in your favor by considering the following points before you start.

- **What do you like to do?** If you hate jogging, you won't be able to maintain a program based on jogging no matter how good it is for you. Don't expect to change your likes and dislikes, especially when starting out.
- **What kind of setting works for you?** Do you have easy access to a pool? If not, swimming probably isn't a good choice. Likewise, if you live in a particularly hot or cold climate, certain outdoor activities may not be sustainable. On the other hand, if there's a network of biking and jogging trails near your office, a routine of lunchtime exercise might be just the ticket.
- **Do you like exercising alone or with others?** Many people find the solitude of swimming or running ideal for contemplation. Others enjoy the motivation and support of a group aerobics class or the company of a walking companion.
- **How much money do you want to spend?** You'll need to weigh expense against other factors, such as the ability to exercise indoors or to participate in a particular activity. Many exercise options are available at a range of prices. You can get great workouts for virtually no money by walking, running, or hiking. A set of inexpensive home barbells can produce the same results as a health club membership. However, some people may find that the money they spend

for gym privileges is a motivating factor. Only you know what will work best in your particular case. But it may take some trial and error to figure it out.

- **What's your current level of fitness?** If you've been sedentary for a while, it's unrealistic (not to mention dangerous) to attempt a five-mile run your first day out. One of the quickest ways to sabotage an exercise program is with an injury. A more practical approach would be to start with walking and work up to greater levels of intensity as your level of fitness increases. If you've had previous injuries or suffer from a chronic disease, talk to your doctor about your physical limitations before deciding on a type of exercise.

- **How can you stay motivated?** To be successful, exercise has to be thoroughly integrated into your lifestyle; it should be something you do as routinely as eating, sleeping, and taking your morning shower. Unfortunately, that can be difficult, as you may already know. The information that follows may help you stay on course when your motivation starts to flag. Remember, the result is worth the effort.

Sticking with Exercise

The value of maintaining an exercise program is evident in the 1993 results of the Harvard Alumni Health Study, published in the *New England Journal of Medicine.* The men who had been moderately active but later became sedentary had a 15 percent higher risk of death over an eight-year period than their counterparts who had never been active. On the other hand, those who started and kept up an exercise program later in life had a 23 percent lower risk of death, which approaches the 29 percent decrease in risk enjoyed by the men who'd always been active. But knowing the intrinsic benefits of lifelong exercise or even creating a personal exercise plan will be of little use if you don't stick to your program. As you plan an exercise routine, you need to prepare for the challenges that await you so you won't be thrown off track.

Set Some Goals

Making an overnight change from a sedentary lifestyle to regular exercise isn't in the cards for most people. What's more, unrealistic expectations will set you up for frustration and failure.

A better approach is to first set a long-term goal, for example, losing twenty-five pounds over the coming year. But because this goal can be daunting when you think about it as a whole, break it into weekly or monthly targets. To drop twenty-five pounds in a year, you'll need to lose just over two pounds a month. Because it takes a deficit of about thirty-five hundred calories to lose a pound, you would need to walk about seventy miles a month (one mile burns roughly one hundred calories). Walking briskly (four miles per hour), you can accomplish that goal with six forty-five-minute walks a week. This is, of course, provided you don't make any changes in your diet or cut back on the amount of other physical activity you get.

Chart Your Progress

Once you've set your goal, you can begin to measure your performance. Record how much you exercised each day in a daily planner or make a simple chart that you can post on the refrigerator. Use Figure 7.2 to keep track of your progress. The sense of accomplishment you get from writing down your exercise can be a big motivator, as can looking back over your logs and seeing how far you've come.

Reward Your Efforts

Meeting your exercise goals, even short-term ones, is cause for celebration. It reflects your commitment to improving your health. Find ways to pat yourself on the back. Whether your reward is small or large, make sure it's something meaningful and enjoyable. Rewards to avoid are those things that you may regret soon after, such as eating an ice cream cone if your ultimate goal is losing weight. A better choice might be a new CD to listen to while you walk.

FIGURE 7.2 Workout Calendar

Month:

Sunday	Monday	Tuesday	Wednesday	Thursday	Friday	Saturday
Time: Activity:	Time: Activity:	Time: Activity:	Time: Activity:	Time: Activity:	Time: Activity:	Time: Activity:
Time: Activity:	Time: Activity:	Time: Activity:	Time: Activity:	Time: Activity:	Time: Activity:	Time: Activity:
Time: Activity:	Time: Activity:	Time: Activity:	Time: Activity:	Time: Activity:	Time: Activity:	Time: Activity:
Time: Activity:	Time: Activity:	Time: Activity:	Time: Activity:	Time: Activity:	Time: Activity:	Time: Activity:
Time: Activity:	Time: Activity:	Time: Activity:	Time: Activity:	Time: Activity:	Time: Activity:	Time: Activity:

Getting Back on Track

Even the most dedicated exercisers sometimes go astray. Almost anything can knock you off track: a bad cold, an out-of-town trip, or a stretch of bad weather. That's why it's critical to learn how to reclaim your routine. When you've missed workout sessions, you need to evaluate your current level of fitness and set goals accordingly. If you've been away from your routine for two weeks or more, don't expect to start where you left off. Cut your workout in half for the first few days to give your body time to readjust.

The bigger challenge may come in getting yourself back in an exercise frame of mind. Try to keep confidence in yourself when you relapse. Instead of expending energy on feeling guilty and defeated, focus on what it'll take to get started again. Once you resume your program, you'll be amazed at how quickly it will begin to feel natural. Here are a few tricks you might try to rekindle your motivation:

- Imagine yourself exercising. Recall the aspects of exercise you enjoy most.
- Come up with a tantalizing reward to give yourself when you meet your first goal after resuming your program.
- Line up exercise partners for your next few outings.
- If completing your whole exercise routine seems overwhelming, mentally divide it into smaller chunks, and give yourself the option of stopping at the end of each one. However, when you reach a checkpoint, encourage yourself to move on to the next one instead of quitting.
- Rather than focus on why you don't want to exercise, concentrate on how good you feel when you've finished a workout.

CHAPTER 8

Drug Treatment

For some people, no matter how strictly they stick to their diet and exercise program, they just can't get their LDL low enough. Others with very high heart disease risk might need immediate drug therapy to get their levels to a safe zone. If you're one of these people, you have quite a few options.

Cholesterol treatment has changed dramatically over my lifetime as a physician. When I was a medical student in the 1970s, we knew that high cholesterol levels were a risk factor for coronary disease, but we did not measure cholesterol levels often, even in people who had heart attacks, and we treated people with high cholesterol even less often. Why? Because we did not have any proof that lowering high cholesterol levels would make a difference to a patient's health. We also didn't have drugs that were very good at bringing the numbers down.

The two types of drugs available in the 1970s are still used today (niacin and bile/cholesterol–binding resins), but they typically lower LDL cholesterol by only 10 percent to 20 percent, and they have many side effects. In 1987, the first statin, lovastatin (Mevacor), was approved and the cholesterol world changed. At its highest dose, lovastatin could lower LDL cholesterol values about 40 percent, and it could be taken as a single, small pill, once a day. Side effects were minimal. The development of lovastatin launched the cholesterol-treatment era, and we have been targeting lower and lower LDLs, with stronger and stronger statins, ever since. Although practices may vary, the decision to treat with a statin is generally based on the National Cholesterol Education Panel guidelines for LDL treatment that were reviewed earlier in the book.

In this chapter, I'll discuss the popular treatments for cholesterol, as well as how to stick with your medication routine.

Reductase Inhibitors (Statins)

Statins are the most widely used class of cholesterol-lowering drugs. Large, randomized clinical trials have shown—and continue to show—that people who use statins have a 20 percent to 40 percent reduction in death from incidents of major cardiac events in studies lasting two to six years.

The study that really brought statins into the limelight was called the Scandinavian Simvastatin Survival Study, or the 4S trial. It involved 4,444 men and women, ages thirty-five to seventy, who had preexisting heart disease and high total cholesterol levels. Half took the cholesterol-lowering drug simvastatin for five years, and half took placebo tablets containing no medication. By the end of the trial, LDL levels in the treatment group had fallen by 35 percent and total cholesterol dropped by 25 percent, while no change took place in the placebo group. The treatment group also had a 30 percent lower chance of dying during the trial and a 34 percent lower chance of having a major coronary event (a nonfatal heart attack or death from coronary heart disease).

Other studies that proved statins' effectiveness in other populations followed in relatively short order. While the 4S participants all had preexisting heart disease, the 6,595 men who volunteered for the West of Scotland Coronary Prevention Study did not, though they did have high cholesterol. Those who took a statin (this time one called pravastatin) lowered their LDL and total cholesterol levels by 26 percent and 20 percent, respectively, and their risk of having a major coronary event by 31 percent, compared with those who took placebo tablets.

Telling Good Studies from Bad

An informed patient is in a much better position to partner with his or her physician to achieve optimal health. However, medical news can be misleading or hard to understand, and a little knowledge can indeed prove to be a dangerous thing. Even doctors can get caught up in promising preliminary studies and jump to false conclusions. So what can you do? What follows is a primer on interpreting medical news.

- **Randomized controlled study.** This is the gold standard of medical research. It means that researchers took a group of people and randomly gave some of them a therapy (a medication or prescription for a lifestyle change, for example) and gave the others (the control group) a placebo and compared the two results.
- **Placebo.** This is a fake treatment. If a controlled study is trying to determine whether a medication works, researchers will give the control group a fake pill so that subjects don't know if they're receiving the real thing. This is important because people's minds can influence outcomes in important ways. Simply thinking that you are getting treated with something can often make you better.
- **Observational study.** This is the kind of study where researchers observe people as they live their lives and then draw conclusions. For example, researchers might ask people to write down everything they eat and their daily weight. From that data, researchers would draw conclusions about what kind of diets cause weight loss. In other cases, researchers work retrospectively—asking people to look back at their lives and note their lifestyles or drug treatments and their health problems.

  Though these kinds of studies can be helpful, they have their flaws. For example, unless researchers in the previous example also observed the patients' exercise habits and

(continued)

Telling Good Studies from Bad, *continued*

measured their metabolisms, the results could be skewed. With retrospective studies, problems often occur because it's extremely difficult for researchers to find a comparison group that is the same in every way as the group they've chosen to observe.

A real-life example of the problems of observational studies is what happened with hormone replacement therapy (HRT). The data suggesting that HRT was good for the heart was based on observational studies. When HRT was put to a randomized controlled test, the old thinking was reversed. How could this be? We now assume that the women in the observational studies who took HRT also had healthier lifestyles that contributed to the fact that they suffered fewer heart problems.

- **Preliminary data.** Before a company or the government will fund a large, expensive trial (some of them run into the millions of dollars), they want to see preliminary data that support the researchers' hypothesis. Retrospective studies are done first, because they are cheaper. However, their results may not hold up when the larger prospective study is finally done. This is exactly what happened with hormone replacement therapy. The retrospective studies made HRT look great, but the randomized, prospective study showed no benefit.

Then came the Cholesterol and Recurrent Events (CARE) trial. This study of pravastatin therapy involved 4,159 people who had recently had heart attacks but whose LDL cholesterol levels were only modestly elevated (the average was 140–150 mg/dL). Compared to subjects in the control group, those taking pravastatin for five years were less likely to have a stroke or a second heart attack or need a procedure to open a clogged artery.

Characteristics of Good Studies

A good study is generally done for a reasonable amount of time, though "reasonable" changes meanings depending on the study. Cholesterol levels in the blood fall to their lowest point after about six weeks on statins, so a yearlong study does not need to be done to determine how well a statin lowers LDL cholesterol. If, however, you are interested in the prevention of strokes or heart attacks, it typically takes two or more years of treatment to see a statin's effects.

A study also has to have a large number of patients. If a group is big enough, and you divide them in two, they should look alike in most ways. This isn't the case in small groups. Before a good study is conducted, statisticians are called in to estimate how many people have to be in the study to make it reliable.

When you're reading about studies, note the population in which they are done. If the study is on white males and you're a Latino woman, the results may not apply to you. The same goes for if the study was conducted on patients who have already had a heart attack and you haven't.

Finally, most journals now require authors to report any financial conflicts that could have tainted their judgment in the work they are reporting. While this is intended to eliminate the most flagrant and unethical behavior, it also alerts reviewers of the work to look for unintentional biases that might have crept into the report.

In the space of just four years, these large studies marshaled powerful evidence of the value of statin drugs in lowering cholesterol. And more studies continue to confirm this. The Heart Protection Study published in 2002, for example, studied the effect of simvastatin versus placebo in more than twenty thousand people in Great Britain with heart disease or diabetes, but with low enough LDL levels that statins would not necessarily be prescribed. Half were randomly chosen to receive simvastatin, the other half placebo. The ten thousand people receiving simvastatin had 18 percent fewer deaths from cardiovascular events and a 25 percent reduction in first heart attacks and stroke over the five years of the study. Even more recently, other studies have shown the benefit of lowering cholesterol levels lower than was previously recommended.

These and other studies demonstrated that statins reduce the risk of having a heart attack or other major coronary event for almost everyone—people with and without preexisting heart disease and those with high cholesterol, borderline-high cholesterol, and even normal cholesterol. This has prompted some to suggest that almost everyone should be taking a statin, and the United Kingdom has recently approved the sale of a statin as an over-the-counter drug. Should everyone be on a statin? The answer is no. First, statins are not approved for use in women who are pregnant because they may cause fetal damage. Second, statins have side effects that, while rare, are serious. Third, statins are expensive, and many people can achieve acceptable levels of coronary disease risk without using medications at all. So, I think the message physicians should be bringing to their patients is not that everyone should be on a statin but rather that everyone should know their heart disease risks and be treated if those risks warrant it. A lot more people should probably be on statins than are currently taking them, but these drugs are definitely not for everyone.

How Do Statins Work?

Statins reduce the amount of cholesterol the liver makes by blocking the key protein needed in that process, HMG CoA reductase (3-hydroxy-3-methylglutaryl-coenzyme A reductase). With less cholesterol made in the liver (and remember that we typically make about 70 percent of the cholesterol in our bodies), the liver tries to recapture more of the LDL cholesterol in the circulation. When it does this by removing LDL particles from the blood, the blood LDL cholesterol level drops (see Figure 8.1). Statins tend to

¡FIGURE 8.1 Liver Cell as Cholesterol Factory

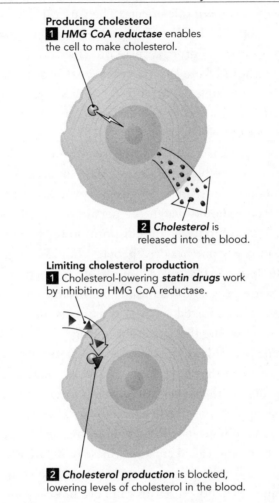

Producing cholesterol
1 *HMG CoA reductase* enables the cell to make cholesterol.

2 *Cholesterol* is released into the blood.

Limiting cholesterol production
1 Cholesterol-lowering *statin drugs* work by inhibiting HMG CoA reductase.

2 *Cholesterol production* is blocked, lowering levels of cholesterol in the blood.

Most of the cholesterol circulating in your blood has been made by your liver, not digested from the food you eat. An enzyme called HMG CoA reductase plays a key role in deciding how much cholesterol the liver makes.

work a little better when taken with your evening meal because cholesterol synthesis is higher at night, but all of the statins can be taken once a day, even in the morning, and still work quite well. The longest-acting statins, like atorvastatin, stay in the body so long that it really doesn't matter when you take the pill.

Side Effects

Statins have few known side effects. They are capable of damaging the liver and muscles, but such problems are rare and usually not serious. One statin drug, cerivastatin (Baycol), however, was voluntarily removed from the market in 2001 because its use was associated with multiple occurrences of rhabdomyolysis, a condition characterized by muscle cell damage that can lead to kidney failure and, very rarely, death.

Rhabdomyolysis is a potential adverse effect of all statin drugs, and the risk seems to be significantly higher in patients who take statins in combination with fibrate drugs. If you take this duo, you and your doctor should watch for persistent muscle aches and pains, which could indicate a predisposition to rhabdomyolysis. About five of every one hundred people who take a statin report having muscle pain. However, not all of these complaints are because of statins. It sounds confusing, but in large trials on statins, muscle pain was reported by nearly as many people taking a placebo as were taking the active statin drug.

Still, some people have muscle aches right after starting a statin that go away when they stop taking it. About eight of every ten thousand people who take a statin develop severe muscle pain or weakness. Stopping the drug almost always makes the problem disappear. Some physicians routinely measure the levels of muscle protein in the blood, called creatine kinase (CK or CPK), to look for early signs of statin-induced muscle injury. I don't find the test of much value. Patients on statins can have muscle pains without CK elevations, and they can have CK elevations in the absence of muscle pain, even when not taking a statin. Asking patients about their muscle symptoms has been the best way for me to determine if the statin is causing a problem. If we are unsure, we stop the drug for a while and see what happens. The blood test can't give a definite answer, but, most often, a careful conversation between the doctor and the patient can.

Another potential effect of statins is an alteration in the liver function tests. This side effect is the one that most patients have heard of and the one they worry about the most. This worry is unwarranted, in my opinion. Up to two of every one hundred people who take a statin have higher-than-normal blood levels of liver proteins called transaminases (pronounced trans-AM-eh-nase). It's not clear if a small increase signals a real problem. An American Heart Association advisory on statin safety calls statin-caused liver failure "exceedingly rare." While I think it is prudent to have a liver test done about once a year when taking a statin, that may be more cautious than necessary. Elevated liver transaminases caused by statins usually revert to normal in days or weeks after stopping the drug, so even an abnormal set of liver tests is no cause for alarm.

Statins can also make people drowsy, constipated, or nauseated, but these side effects are quite uncommon. The United Kingdom even recently decided that one statin, simvastatin, was safe enough that it could be provided as an over-the-counter (nonprescription) drug. The U.S. Food and Drug Administration is reviewing that option for several statins in this country. (I'll talk about this further in Chapter 11.)

Because statins are relatively new medications, it's hard to know for sure what the statins' long-term effects will be. Long-term studies on statins are critical because people will probably take these drugs for decades. The first such analysis offers some reassurance. A decade-long study from Sweden showed that the side effects of simvastatin (Zocor) were limited to minor, temporary changes in liver enzymes circulating in the bloodstream. My own view is that if seventeen years of widespread use have failed to reveal any seriously troubling news about this class of drugs, it is unlikely that something bad will emerge in the future. The relatively high risk of coronary disease in most middle-aged and older Americans tips the scale in favor of long-term statin use. For most teenagers and young adults, the risk of coronary disease in the short term is lower, making it reasonable to treat these younger folks less aggressively most of the time.

It is important to note that statins have been shown to cause fetal malformations in embryos of test animals, so no woman of childbearing age should take the drugs without taking measures to avoid pregnancy. For these reasons, I tend not to treat women under thirty or thirty-five with statins unless they have extraordinarily elevated LDL cholesterol levels or a striking family history of early coronary artery disease.

Pluses

Besides the obvious—their powerful cholesterol-lowering ability—my patients also like that statins require only one daily dose, which makes it easier for people to remember to take them correctly. Statins also don't interact with most of the other drugs heart patients commonly take, including antiangina medications (beta-blockers, calcium channel blockers, nitrates), antihypertensive medications (diuretics, angiotensin class inhibitors), or antiarrhythmics.

Choosing Your Statin

While statins have worked wonders for many people, they've also made a lot of money for drug companies. And as new statins come out, those companies are going to work hard to recruit you to their side. So how can you tell which statin is right for you and what's just marketing hype? First, realize that all statins lower cholesterol by the same mechanism, so they all lower LDL and triglycerides and boost HDL cholesterol a small amount, though they differ in degree in all of these things. The members of the statin family also share similar major side effects. Second, note their differences:

- **Ingredients.** Each brand-name statin differs from the others in that it has a unique chemical structure. The statin pills also contain distinctive inactive ingredients used to hold it together, preserve it, and get it into the bloodstream. These variances can cause the body to handle each drug differently. If you have a side effect on one brand of statin, it does not guarantee that you will have the same side effect on a different brand.

Taking Your Medicine Correctly

I know that life can interfere with a medication schedule. It can be easy to forget to stick to your schedule if you're out of your normal routine or if you're just busy. However, it's important that you try to remember to take your medications regularly and that you don't stop taking a medication without talking to your doctor first. Medication is prescribed in a certain dose to be taken at certain intervals for a reason: to ensure that it does its job.

I hope these numbers will shock you into staying on track: an observational study published in the *Pharmaceutical Journal* in 2004 found that 25 percent of people prescribed a statin did not refill their prescriptions regularly or at all. These people were two and a half times more likely to have a heart event than those who complied with their doctor's orders.

Why did people not take their meds? A small percentage of people complained of side effects, but the authors hypothesize that a lot of patients find it hard to stick with long-term therapy that isn't making them feel any different immediately. After all, until your arteries get seriously clogged with cholesterol, you can't really feel that you have a problem. But people with high cholesterol do have a major problem, and those on medication need to take it according to their doctor's orders in order to prevent heart problems.

My patients have found lots of ways to help them remember their medication and stay motivated. You can try these or come up with something that works for you.

- Statins are usually taken with your evening meal. Let something you do right before you eat—set the table, wash your hands— act as a reminder to get out your medication. You can do the same thing with medications taken at any time of day. Use brushing your teeth for cues at night or in the morning, for example.

(continued)

Taking Your Medicine Correctly, *continued*

- Set the timer on your watch to go off when you're supposed to take your medication.
- Tell those around you to remind you.
- Create a chart or use the one in Figure 8.2 to keep the information about your medications organized and in one place.
- Remember that with a chronic condition like high cholesterol, the medication is working even if you don't feel any different after taking it. If you're tempted to stop, discuss this with your doctor.

Though it's good to take responsibility for your health, doctors aren't off the hook here either. The study previously mentioned found that people who had their cholesterol monitored frequently were more likely to comply with their doctor's orders—possibly because of the feedback showing them that the medication was working. For that reason, I try to see all of my patients twice a year, and I ask that they get a lipid panel done before coming in to see me so we can discuss the results. For those whose insurance won't cover a second trip to the doctor's office for a prevention visit, I get the blood work and report the results over the phone. Seeing a doctor to discuss your cholesterol results every year can reinforce the importance of taking your medication, allow you to address any side effects you're experiencing, and help keep you on that diet and exercise program. Talk to your doctor about how often you should follow up with appointments and cholesterol tests.

- **Potency.** Some statins are more potent than others, meaning that the same dose lowers cholesterol by different amounts. A 20 mg tablet of Pravachol, for example, lowers LDL by 24 percent on average, while a 20 mg tablet of Lipitor lowers it by 46 percent. But potency doesn't matter as much as the medication's efficacy—the maximum

FIGURE 8.2 My Medication Chart

Medication	Why I Take It	When I Take It	My Dose	What to Avoid While on This Med.	Major Side Effects	What to Do if I Have Side Effects	Miscellaneous
Example: Lipitor	high cholesterol	with dinner	40mg	nothing	muscle pain	call Dr. Brown	refill on 1st of month

amount a statin can lower LDL at its highest FDA-approved dose. Lipitor used to be strongest, but now it has to share this honor with Crestor. Remember, though, that you don't necessarily need to pick the strongest statin if a "weaker" one gets you to your target LDL level.

- **Proof of benefits.** Four of the statins—Mevacor, Pravachol, Zocor, and Lipitor—have been tested the most in large clinical trials showing that the drugs prevented heart attacks and deaths from heart disease. There is less proof that Lescol and Crestor do the same thing, but most experts believe that the benefits of statins are shared across the six drugs.

- **Cost.** You can pay anywhere between $35 and $120 for a month's worth of statin tablets (see Table 8.1). Which statin will be least expensive for you can depend on your health insurance. Because all the statins seem to be beneficial, it's reasonable to pick the cheapest one that gets you to your target LDL level. The first statin approved, lovastatin, is now available generically, and simvastatin and pravastatin will soon follow, so these will all likely be cheaper alternatives to brand-name-only statins.

- **Side effects.** Statins' unwanted side effects fall into four main camps: liver changes, muscle pain, interactions with drugs and food, and everything else. The first two, as noted earlier, are nearly the same for all the statins. The others aren't necessarily. That's because the liver uses one set of reactions to break down Mevacor, Zocor, and Lipitor; a different set for Lescol and Crestor; and yet another for Pravachol. Drugs or foods that block these reactions can boost statin levels in the blood, while drugs that rev up the process can lower statin levels. Grapefruit juice, for example, increases blood levels of Mevacor, Zocor, and Lipitor but doesn't usually affect the others. But it takes a lot of grapefruit juice to make this difference matter, so it may be an important factor for only a few individuals who drink unusually large amounts of it.

TABLE 8.1 Comparing the Statins

Brand Name	Generic Name	Usual Starting Dose (Percent Reduction in LDL)	Maximum Dose (Percent Reduction in LDL)	Cost of a Month's Supply
Mevacor*	lovastatin	20 mg (29 percent)	80 mg (48 percent)	10 mg, $32; 20 mg, $37; 40 mg, $63
Pravachol	pravastatin	20 mg (24 percent)	80 mg (37 percent)	10 and 20 mg, $83; 40 mg, $120; 80 mg, $130
Zocor	simvastatin	20 mg (35 percent)	80 mg (46 percent)	5 mg, $54; 10 mg, $70; 20, 40, and 80 mg, $124
Lescol	fluvastatin	20 mg (17 percent)	80 mg (36 percent)	20 and 40 mg, $54; 80 mg, $68
Lipitor	atorvastatin	10 mg (38 percent)	80 mg (54 percent)	10 mg, $63; 20, 40, and 80 mg, $95
Crestor	rosuvastatin	10 mg (45 percent)	40 mg (63 percent)	5, 10, and 20 mg, $70; 40 mg, $76

*Also available as a generic for about half the price listed, except the 20 mg dose, which is about $10 cheaper.

Source: Prices from drugstore.com, on 9/2/2004

People taking statins have reported constipation, upset stomach, dizziness, trouble sleeping, rashes, and even hair loss. Because these could be reactions to a specific statin, changing to a different one may help. If not, you may need to switch to another type of cholesterol-lowering drug, such as niacin, colesevelam (WelChol), or ezetimibe (Zetia). I personally tried three statins before I found one that I could take without side effects. I believed in the value of taking one enough that I was willing to try several to find one I could take without a problem.

The choice of which statin to take—assuming it is appropriate to take one—has traditionally been made by your doctor. However, you are entitled to ask why he or she chose one statin over the others. There may be an equally effective and less expensive alternative, which most doctors are happy to prescribe if they are asked to consider it.

Patient Story: One of These Drugs Is Not Like the Others One Saturday morning, as was her habit, Elizabeth was feeding the ducks at a local pond. As she was enjoying this weekend ritual, she noticed she wasn't feeling very well. "I started to feel awful and thought, 'What's going on?' I decided I should walk back to the car. When I got there, my hands and arms were white. I knew that meant blood wasn't flowing to my arms. I said to myself, 'Elizabeth, you've got to get yourself to a hospital.' I got in the car, and by the time I reached the emergency room driveway, I felt so ill that I just leaned on the horn until someone came to help."

Elizabeth's years working at Massachusetts General Hospital may have helped save her life. She recognized that her symptoms were a sign of serious trouble. As with many women who have heart attacks, chest pain wasn't even part of the picture. The most common warning signs of a heart attack in women include weakness, unusual fatigue, a cold sweat, dizziness, nausea, and a heavy or weak feeling in the arms. Elizabeth knew she needed medical help immediately. While generally it isn't a good idea to drive yourself to the hospital if you think you're having a heart attack, Elizabeth knew she had to do something. "I knew I just had to deal with it."

But there were ominous signs of potential heart disease risk that didn't quite sink in. "Eleven years ago when I had my heart attack, I didn't think much about cholesterol. My sister had had a massive heart attack at age forty-two, but I thought I was exempt. I became, 'enlightened,' shall I say." As she recovered from her heart attack, Elizabeth learned that her cholesterol level was 489, with an LDL of 400.

When I first saw Elizabeth, I started her on a statin, but it didn't give us a great result. "My cholesterol only came down to the 300s," recalls Elizabeth. "I've probably tried every statin made. None of them really got my cholesterol down very far, and they all, and one in particular, gave me terrible muscle aches, mostly in my legs. Niacin caused terrible stomach upset. For a while, I took Questran, which I mixed into Jell-O. I even tried a vegetarian diet, but my cholesterol went up! I was at my wit's end."

Elizabeth's primary care doctor was concerned enough that she kept Elizabeth on a very low dose of hormone replacement therapy, hoping it might help control blood lipids a little. At an office visit in late 2003, Elizabeth and I talked about trying the new statin, Crestor. We started with 5 mg/day. According to Elizabeth, "The result was dramatic. For the first time my cholesterol was in the low 200s and my LDL in the 100s. I thought to myself, 'OK, if we go up to 10 mg/day and stop the hormones, let's see what happens.' And that seemed to do it. I was so happy, I felt like telling the world."

People often eye drug companies with suspicion, assuming that profits are the sole motive for developing "copycat" drugs. But there *are* differences among the statins. Not only do they vary in their properties—for example, they are not all metabolized the same way and this might influence which statin to try first—but not every drug in a given class will work for every person. What is so striking about Elizabeth's story is that she tried five statins, none of which worked for her and all of which caused significant side effects. With such a dangerously high LDL, there was too much at stake to give up. We have now found one—at least so far—that she can take.

Many doctors and patients give up after trying one or two statins but shouldn't because a little more trial and error might reveal an effective and well-tolerated therapy. What works well in one person may not work well in another. A drug that causes mild or no side effects in one person may trigger debilitating or serious side effects in her neighbor. The bottom line is that you'll need to work with your doctor to find the drug (or drugs) and dose that works for you with minimal side effects.

Elizabeth's persistence and thoughtful approach to lowering her cholesterol eventually paid off. Her last test results showed an LDL cholesterol level less than 130—pretty impressive for someone whose untreated LDL is above 400. It was a great moment for both of us. I told her that we should frame her lab report.

Today, Elizabeth says that, apart from some nagging arthritis and minor muscle aches, she's feeling good. She pays close attention to her cardiovascular health, and her doctors monitor the vessels in her neck and legs, which show some signs of atherosclerosis. What would she tell someone who is struggling to lower cholesterol with little success? "Hang in there," she says. "It was really a challenge, but I thought if I don't do something, this is going to get me. I'll die of cardiovascular disease." The importance of family history isn't lost on Elizabeth either. "My boys run high cholesterol, too," she reports. "Some are treating it; others are ignoring it, but I preach at them."

Elizabeth is clearly a woman of strength and resolve. I know she will keep after her sons about getting their cholesterol under control because she has clearly seen the benefit of it to her own health. Doing so can be especially tough for some people, but it's worth the effort.

Should You Take a High-Dose Statin?

In 2004, before and after the NCEP issued its guidelines, questions arose about high-dose statins. In one of the studies that the NCEP cited as evidence behind issuing the lower optional LDL goal for people at the highest risk, the people who got their LDL levels below 100 were taking a high-dose statin. That led many people to start wondering if they should take the same. My philosophy is that it's safest to start on the lowest dose that you and your doctor think will give you heart benefits and then adjust upward if need be. Why? The higher the statin dose, the higher the risk of side effects.

Statins: Not Only for Cholesterol

Though statins are prescribed for their cholesterol-lowering power, as more people take them, we're finding that they may help with other things, too. Doctors won't prescribe statins for any of the following problems just yet, but that may change in the future.

- **Alzheimer's disease.** A series of observational studies has linked statin use with a reduced risk (of 39 percent to 74 percent) of Alzheimer's disease and other forms of dementia. Because damage to blood vessels can cause age-related memory loss, it makes sense that lowering cholesterol may help prevent it. And the drugs may even protect brain cells as well as the arteries that nourish them. A 2002 German study indicates that the statins can enter these cells, affecting cholesterol metabolism in the brain itself. Scientists speculate that the statins may even reduce the brain's production of beta-amyloid, the protein that causes much of the damage in Alzheimer's disease.
- **Cancer.** A number of studies have shown that statins might prevent colon and prostate cancers. Others have suggested an increased risk of breast cancer linked to statin use, and still others have shown no effect. Though the evidence is obviously far from conclusive, researchers have come up with a few theories of how statins might stop some cancers. One is that statins stop activation of the proteasome, a complex of enzymes that chops up proteins like a little cellular garbage disposal. If the proteasome isn't working right, the garbage piles up, and the cells die off instead of proliferating. Other research suggests that statins block various "go" signs in intracellular signaling pathways that rev up cancerous cell division. And sometimes their good old cholesterol-lowering effects may come into play. A study published in 2003 found that statins kill off the acute myelogenous leukemia cells that seem to need high cholesterol levels to survive.
- **Multiple sclerosis (MS).** A small study indicated that an 80 mg dose of simvastatin may reduce the progression of multiple sclerosis in people with a kind known as relapsing-remitting. Researchers think statins' power to fight inflammation might be the reason behind this finding.
- **Osteoporosis.** In animal experiments, statins helped form new bone. Several studies in people suggest that these drugs

may prevent osteoporosis and broken bones. However, others haven't shown the same effect.

- **Kidney function.** A large 2004 study indicated that the kidney function of people with heart disease and high cholesterol declines as time goes by. Patients in the study treated with a statin, however, didn't see this decline. What's more, those whose kidney function was starting to decline saw a reversal of this development.
- **CRP levels.** It's known that statins lower C-reactive protein levels. Keep in mind that we're still not sure whether lowering them helps combat heart troubles.
- **Stroke.** A few studies have noted the 25 percent lowered stroke risk that comes along with taking a statin. Some strokes are caused by changes in the walls of the arteries leading to the brain similar to the changes in the arteries to the heart that cause a heart attack. Statins' effects on the arteries may be the same whether they're in the heart or brain.
- **Peripheral artery disease.** An effect of narrowed arteries, this disease causes cramps, numbness, or tingling in the legs and buttocks when a person walks. In a study of almost four hundred people with peripheral artery disease, people who were taking a statin could walk farther and faster without problems than those who weren't.
- **Other heart benefits.** Aggressive cholesterol-lowering therapy, with or without statins, has also been shown to slow the buildup of fatty plaque inside arteries and even, in some cases, to reduce it. Statins may also stop the buildup of calcium deposits on the heart's "exit valve." Known as aortic stenosis, this narrowing can cause chest pain, dizziness, fatigue, and breathlessness.

Other Drugs

Though statins get most of the press, there are other cholesterol-lowering drugs that may work better for you, or you may need to use a statin in combination with another drug to get to a desired cholesterol level.

Niacin

The B vitamin niacin, also called nicotinic acid, is an essential part of a healthy diet. But at very high daily doses—1,500–4,500 mg—crystalline nicotinic acid acts as a drug instead of a vitamin. It can reduce total cholesterol levels up to 25 percent, lowering LDL and raising HDL, and can rapidly lower the blood level of triglycerides. It does so by cutting the liver's production of very low-density lipoprotein, which is ordinarily converted into LDL. Because niacin has been around since the 1950s, it is well studied.

You might be wondering why niacin isn't on top of the cholesterol-lowering hill, instead of statins. There are two main reasons: its side effects and confusion over the different types of niacin out there.

The original niacin preparations used for lowering cholesterol were pure crystalline nicotinic acid, which enters the bloodstream quickly. Appropriately, it is called fast-acting or immediate-release niacin. The quick spike in niacin triggers a "niacin flush" in almost everyone who isn't used to this drug. This uncomfortable feeling of heat, itching, tingling, or redness in the skin starts within a few minutes of taking niacin and subsides within an hour or so. Less common side effects are gastrointestinal upset (such as queasiness, heartburn, or gas) and dizziness or light-headedness, especially when rising from bed or a chair.

To minimize flushing and other side effects, several companies have developed extended-release formulations of niacin. Like timed-release cold capsules, these deliver a steady stream of niacin over several hours. By avoiding a surge in nicotinic acid in the bloodstream, these lessen—but don't eliminate—flushing. There's a downside, though. Because blood levels of niacin stay high all day long, the liver never gets a break from processing niacin, as it does with immediate-release niacin that quickly leaves the body. This can overwhelm the liver and has led to numerous cases of liver problems, including liver failure requiring a transplant.

Importance of Diet Even with Drugs

Though this chapter focuses on drug therapy, that's not to say that
everyone—even those on cholesterol medication—shouldn't
implement the lifestyle changes mentioned in Chapters 6 and 7.
Though drugs can work wonders on cholesterol levels, they work
best if used as part of a heart-healthy lifestyle. An observational
study in the *Journal of the American College of Cardiology* in 2003
reinforced this.

At the University of Texas Medical School, researchers followed
more than four hundred men and women with chest pain (angina)
or other forms of coronary artery disease. Some of them did little to
control their cholesterol levels. Others gave cholesterol control a
decent try by taking a statin and following a standard heart-healthy
diet, or by following a very strict diet. Those in a third group went
all out: they adopted a strict diet, exercised, and took a statin.

The all-out approach was the clear champion (see Figure 8.3).
During the five-year study, only one in twenty of the people in this
group had a heart attack, underwent a procedure to open or
bypass cholesterol-narrowed arteries, or died of heart disease.
Rates of such cardiovascular problems ballooned in the medium-
effort and do-nothing groups.

Tests that could look at the coronary arteries done at the study's
start and again two to three years later showed much the same

An intermediate-release form that's available only by prescription seems to offer the best of both worlds. This drug, sold as
Niaspan, delivers niacin slower than the original fast-acting types
but faster than the extended-release versions. This, and the fact
that it's taken once a day at bedtime, helps minimize flushing, or
at least the experience of it. Because it is washed out of the body
in a few hours, it is easier on the liver than extended-release niacin.

Several brands of "no-flush" niacin are also on the market. In
theory, one of its components, inositol hexanicotinate, is absorbed

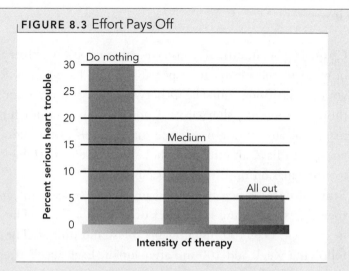

FIGURE 8.3 Effort Pays Off

Intensity of therapy

Percent serious heart trouble

Do nothing

Medium

All out

The more intense the prevention efforts, the smaller the percentage of heart problems.

thing. In the high-effort group, blood flow through the coronary arteries had actually improved, while in the other two groups it continued to decline.

And remember, any cost or side effects involved in taking a medication don't apply to lowering your cholesterol through lifestyle changes.

into the bloodstream, and its niacin components are gradually released. In reality, it barely elevates niacin levels in the blood and barely changes cholesterol levels.

If you have chronic liver disease or certain other conditions, including diabetes, gout, and peptic ulcer, be sure to mention them to your doctor. Niacin might exacerbate them. Everyone on niacin should have their liver function checked occasionally, especially after starting on niacin or changing your dose. People with diabetes should monitor their blood sugar even more carefully when they're on niacin. Here are some other tips for taking niacins.

- **Choosing a niacin.** If you have patience, it's worth trying immediate-release niacin, especially if you have to pay for your medications yourself. Otherwise, Niaspan is a good, though expensive, alternative. I don't recommend no-flush niacin because it doesn't elevate niacin levels in the blood enough to have an effect on cholesterol. Refer to Table 8.2 for information on different niacin types.
- **Start slowly.** When beginning immediate-release niacin therapy, take 100 mg right after dinner for a week. The next week, take 100 mg after breakfast and dinner. The following week add 100 mg after lunch. Each week after that, double the dose at one meal until you reach your daily target.

TABLE 8.2 Comparing Niacin Types

Type	Advantages	Disadvantages	Monthly Cost*
Immediate-release (fast-acting, crystalline)	Used safely for fifty years, shown to prevent heart attacks and premature heart-related death	Causes flushing and may upset the stomach; amount of free niacin differs by brand	$7 to $9.60
Intermediate-release (Niaspan, by prescription only)	Once-a-day, bedtime dosing lets flushing occur during sleep; FDA approved	Hides and minimizes flushing but doesn't eliminate it	$120
Sustained-release (timed, slow, and extended-release)	Less flushing than with immediate-release niacin	Increased risk of liver damage	$13.50 to $16
No-flush	As the name implies, no flushing	Delivers little free niacin; little or no evidence about safety; not effective	$24 to $26

* For 2,000 mg per day, as of 9/2004. Information from *Annals of Internal Medicine* 2003, 139:996–1002, and drugstore.com.

Source: "Don't Overlook Niacin for Treating Cholesterol Problems," *Harvard Heart Letter*, April 2004, page 4.

- **Aspirin helps.** If you can take a full-strength or even low-dose aspirin, or already do, take it each day about thirty minutes before your first dose of niacin. This can dramatically reduce the niacin flush.
- **Eat up.** Taking niacin with or soon after a meal helps prevent digestive irritation. If you plan on having something spicy, take your niacin later, with a less fiery snack.
- **Don't make changes before talking to your doctor.** A switch from immediate-release niacin to extended-release, or vice versa, requires changing the daily dose. Merely changing types can lead to hepatitis or liver failure. Don't increase your dose or take any kind of high-dose niacin, even those sold over the counter, without talking to your doctor.
- **Stop taking the drug if you have the flu or other illness that can tax the liver.** Once you are well, start up again at a lower dose than you had been taking.

Ezetimibe

One of the newest drugs on the cholesterol-lowering block is Zetia (ezetimibe). Like a statin, ezetimibe reduces total cholesterol, LDL cholesterol, and apolipoprotein B, a protein constituent of LDL cholesterol. It works in a different way than statins, though. Instead of interfering with the body's mechanism for making cholesterol, ezetimibe interferes with the body's absorption of dietary cholesterol from the small intestine. Taking ezetimibe along with a statin puts two different mechanisms to work, so it's more effective than taking either drug alone. In the summer of 2004, this got even easier when the drug Vytorin, a combination of ezetimibe and simvastatin, came out. Though doctors had been prescribing this combination of drugs already, Vytorin allows patients to get the two medications in one pill, which can be cheaper and more convenient.

Ezetimibe can also be used as a good alternative for people who can't tolerate statins or other cholesterol-lowering agents, but it is not as effective as any of the statins. We don't have long-term information on its side effects, but there appear to be very few. Some people experience fatigue, stomach pain, or diarrhea.

Fibric Acid Derivatives (Fibrates)

This family of drugs blocks the production and activity of proteins that transport cholesterol. The two that can be prescribed in the United States are gemfibrozil (Lopid) and fenofibrate (Tricor). Fibric acid derivatives are mainly prescribed for people with high triglyceride levels. They reduce triglycerides by 20 percent to 50 percent and raise HDL levels by 10 percent to 15 percent, but they have only a modest effect on LDL.

Gemfibrozil and fenofibrate, which come in pill form, are generally taken once or twice a day with meals. Most people don't experience side effects, although a few develop dyspepsia (feelings of fullness, bloating, or heartburn after eating), dizziness, or changes in sensations such as touch and taste. These drugs can also increase the risk for gallbladder disease and, when used with a statin, can cause rare cases of the muscle-breakdown disorder rhabdomyolysis. They can also boost the effects of blood-thinning drugs such as warfarin (Coumadin).

Though these side effects are uncommon, everyone taking a fibric acid derivative should have their liver function and blood count checked before and during therapy. And people on blood-thinning medications should have their prothrombin time (a measure of clotting ability) monitored closely.

Bile Acid Binders (Resins)

Bile acid binders are synthetic resins that bind chemically with cholesterol-rich bile acids in the intestine, preventing their reabsorption. To replace the bile acids lost in this way, the body draws upon its store of cholesterol, thus lowering cholesterol levels in the blood. Medications in this class include cholestyramine (Prevalite, Questran), colesevelam (WelChol), and colestipol (Colestid). Typically, they lower LDL cholesterol by 15 percent to 30 percent, depending on the daily dose.

Bile acid binders are used much less commonly nowadays because of their many side effects. These include constipation, heartburn, and a bloated feeling. Bile acid binders can also interfere with the action of many drugs, especially digitalis, beta-blockers, warfarin, thiazide diuretics, anticonvulsants, and thyroid hormone supplements. And people with high triglyceride levels should not take this type of medication because it tends to elevate triglycerides. Since ezetimibe has come along, anyone who would've been prescribed bile acid binders will probably get ezetimibe instead.

How to Save Money on Drugs

You don't need the newscasters to tell you that prescription drug prices are on the rise or that insurers are covering less of the cost. For some people, the out-of-pocket outlay for prescription drugs extracts little more than a quiet moan at the cash register. For others, it means skipping medicine or meals in order to pay. Here are some tips for cutting costs.

Get Your Doctor's Help

Unless a doctor knows you're trying to cut corners, he or she won't take price into consideration when filling out the prescription pad. But most doctors are willing and able to help once you mention your concern. Here are a few things to ask about:

- **Generic drugs.** Buying generic drugs instead of the more expensive brand-name versions is one of the most effective ways to cut your monthly drug bill. For example, a month's supply of the 20 mg dose of the brand-name statin Mevacor costs about $70, while the same amount of generic lovastatin costs about $35.

  There's no need to worry that a cheaper price means less quality. The Food and Drug Administration (FDA) regulates the production of generics just as carefully as brand-name drugs. The only difference may be in the inactive ingredients—things like fillers, coatings, and flavorings. Some doctors worry that the inactive ingredients change how much of the active ingredients the body absorbs. The FDA doesn't share this concern, though.

Some classes of drugs are so new that generic forms aren't yet available. If your doctor prescribes one of these, ask if there's a slightly older type of drug that does much the same thing.

- **Cheaper brand-name drugs.** Sometimes you can trade off convenience for savings. For instance, if your doctor suggests a brand-name combination drug, ask if you can save money by taking the component drugs one by one. In other cases, you can save by taking an older drug two or three times a day instead of using a newer (and more expensive) once-a-day formulation.

- **Starting small.** When you start a new drug, ask your doctor to give you a prescription for just a week or two. This way you can see if the dosage is right and if the drug agrees with you. If everything goes well, then you can fill a longer-term prescription. If it doesn't, you aren't stuck with a stockpile of pills you paid for but can't use.

- **Starting low.** Ask about starting a drug at the lowest possible dose, especially for a drug that's relatively new.

- **Splitting the difference.** You expect to pay about twice as much for a two-pound box of pasta as you do for a one-pound box. But the same pricing concept doesn't always apply to drugs. Often, you can save money by asking your doctor to prescribe pills in twice the dosage you need. Then you can cut them in half to double the number of doses. This approach is not for everyone, and it can't be done for all drugs. Capsules and timed-release formulas, in particular, should never be split.

Shop Around for the Best Price

The same kind of comparison shopping you might do for a car or a coffeemaker can pay off for drugs.

- **Buy by mail.** If your prescription drugs are covered by insurance, see if the insurer has a mail-order pharmacy. Some offer lower co-payments.
- **Call around.** You'll find that drug prices vary from store to store. Try independent pharmacies, national chains, and megastores such as Wal-Mart and Costco.
- **Go online.** You can find bargains or quickly compare drug prices on the Internet. (If you don't have a computer, the ones at your public library are free to use, and many librarians will help you find information.) Many brick-and-mortar pharmacies have websites that offer discounts on prescription drugs. So do "virtual" pharmacies, which do all their business online. For the most part, shopping for prescription drugs online is safe. One way to tell if the site is legitimate is the VIPPS (Verified Internet Pharmacy Practice Sites) seal of approval from the National Association of Boards of Pharmacy. You can also check with the board to see if an online pharmacy is licensed and in good standing.

Join a Group

Some organizations offer savings on prescription drugs as a perk. If you're a member of AARP, for example, you can join its MembeRx Choice plan for $20 a year. It offers savings on top-selling drugs. If you served in the military, you may be eligible for the TRICARE Pharmacy or Senior Pharmacy programs. Buying groups such as the Peoples Prescription Plan and the United States Pharmaceutical Group also offer savings and are open to everyone. (Find more information in the Resources.)

Look for Low-Income Options

Some money-saving options are aimed at low- to middle-income seniors without any drug insurance. The Together Rx Card, for example, provides savings on more than 150 widely prescribed medicines. Some states provide assistance with prescription drugs to low-income seniors or people with disabilities who do not qualify for Medicaid. To quickly find out if your state has such a benefit or if you qualify for other programs, try the National Council on the Aging's BenefitsCheckUp Web site. (For more information, see the Resources.)

Reduce Your Need for Drugs

If you're serious about cutting your drug bill, get serious about adopting a healthier lifestyle, which may cut the need for medication. Don't stop taking your pills first and then try to make lifestyle changes. Make the changes first. When you start getting results, *then* talk with your doctor about medication changes.

CHAPTER 9

Treating Other Lipid Problems

Though the majority of people with problem cholesterol have high LDL cholesterol, there are some people whose lipid levels show other abnormalities. The most common of these disorders are elevated blood triglyceride levels or reduced HDL values, both of which can occur with or without high LDL. Low levels of HDL or higher than normal levels of triglyceride increase the likelihood of developing coronary disease, and so they are important to address. They can both be diagnosed by a fasting lipid profile test, and each problem requires a slightly different treatment plan.

Elevated Triglycerides

If you have high triglyceride levels but normal levels of HDL and LDL, one of two things can be to blame: a genetic abnormality or unhealthy lifestyle choices. More commonly, it's the latter. Normal triglyceride levels are less than 150. Levels of 200–1,000 can be caused by having uncontrolled diabetes, being significantly overweight, drinking too much alcohol, or taking certain medications. Medications that affect triglyceride levels include estrogen (either in hormonal replacement regimens or as part of an oral contraceptive), isotretinoin, beta-blockers, thiazide diuretics, and medications that combat HIV.

People with genetic abnormalities that cause their bodies to be unable to metabolize chylomicrons can have triglyceride levels in the thousands. As you might remember from Chapter 1, chylomicrons are 90 percent to 95 percent triglyceride by weight, and they normally get cleared from the bloodstream about twelve hours after eating. If your body can't clear them, triglyceride levels soar.

How dangerous are these high levels? It depends. The extraordinarily high triglyceride levels caused by several of the genetic abnormalities generally do not cause heart disease because it seems that the chylomicron is not prone to producing inflammation in the artery wall, the first step in causing a heart attack. However, it's hard to be confident that heart disease risk for people with triglyceride levels in the thousands is definitely low, because there are relatively few of these people to study and the metabolism of the chylomicron leads to a remnant particle that may cause heart disease.

In any case, very high triglyceride levels can cause other major health problems in the liver and pancreas, so physicians will aggressively treat these patients to lower their triglycerides. In this case, treatment would include a very low-fat diet where only 5 percent to 6 percent of calories come from fat, as opposed to the 20 percent to 30 percent we generally recommend. These individuals also get some benefit from taking fibrate medications, but the effect of the medicines is easily overwhelmed by poor dietary choices.

People with high triglyceride levels caused by lifestyle factors, typically under 1,000 mg/dL, on the other hand, do have an increased risk for heart disease. For women, this increase in risk may be two to two and a half times greater than in women with normal levels, whereas for men the risk appears to be less, about one and a half times. In these cases, the obvious first step is to change the problematic lifestyle. Work with your doctor to treat your diabetes better, switch to a medication that doesn't affect

How High Is Too High for Triglycerides?

Less than 150	Normal
150–199 mg/dL	Borderline-high
200–499 mg/dL	High
500 mg/dL and above	Very high

According to the 2001 NCEP guidelines, people with levels in the borderline, high, or very high groups should get treatment. People who are borderline-high generally start with lifestyle changes, while people in the higher groups normally are told to change their lifestyles and take a fibrate.

triglyceride levels, stop drinking, eat healthier, and exercise. Besides contributing to weight loss, exercise also lowers triglycerides because your muscles use triglycerides as fuel.

If you don't have any of these lifestyle risks or your triglyceride levels don't fall even after you modify your lifestyle, your doctor will probably put you on fibrates.

Patient Story: What a Difference a Diet Makes

My patient Frenchee's story is particularly impressive—so much so that he became the subject of a talk I gave at Harvard Medical School. I first met him about three years ago when routine blood tests showed an "off-the-charts" triglyceride level of 1,400. At that time his blood pressure was 184/110, and at five feet three inches tall and 186 pounds, his weight was a concern and certainly contributing to these problems. I prescribed Lipitor and Tricor to lower Frenchee's cholesterol and triglycerides and also enalapril for his blood pressure. We also talked about his weight, and I had him see the nutritionist in our office.

"I had never really been heavy," explains Frenchee. "My diet wasn't great, but I'd always had physically demanding construction jobs. My weight probably started to creep up when I was in my forties, but it wasn't until I started having trouble bending over to tie my work boots—and was growing into size 38 pants—that I realized it was getting to be a problem."

At his first nutrition consultation he revealed that he drank a two-liter bottle of Coke with dinner every night. Many people don't think of the liquid calories they consume. Almost sheepishly, he admits, "I wouldn't say that I was *addicted* to Coke, but I drank a lot of it. Since I was six years old, I never drank milk, just Coke. I'd have a 20-ounce bottle in the morning, then at lunch, and at breaks." All told, Frenchee was probably drinking about five thousand calories of Coke a day. "The nutritionist suggested that I cut back, but I decided the only thing to do was to go cold turkey. I wasn't sure I could do it, but I did." He also started riding his bike when he had the time. A month later he was nine pounds lighter.

Some of the other recommended dietary changes were nearly as daunting as giving up Coke. But he found ways to change his diet. "I used to have a ham and cheese omelet with home fries for breakfast every morning, with a Coke. I switched to two English muffins with peanut butter in the morning. I couldn't stop for a good lunch, so I decided that would just have to hold me until dinner. By noon I was hungry enough to eat the paper, but I just stuck with it. I discovered turkey and chicken burgers and would eat those for dinner with green beans. Portion control was tough. The diet plan said to have two ounces of meat. I needed more than that to have energy for my job, but I kept my carbohydrate count below the target listed in the diet plan."

By the end of month two, he'd lost eighteen more pounds. After nine months, he'd lost fifty-four pounds. "I bought ten pairs of size 36 jeans and had to return them before I got to wear them. Then I bought ten pairs of size 34 jeans and had to do the same thing." Frenchee now wears a size 32 or 33, depending on the type of jeans. His blood pressure is down to 127/72. He stopped taking Tricor a while ago, when blood tests suggested that triglycerides were below 100. We've cut back on the dose of Lipitor, and he may someday be able to go off it altogether. He has more energy overall and says that tying his work boots is much easier; he's also pleased to report that he can pinch a mere half inch or less around his middle.

When asked what advice he'd give to someone facing a weight-loss challenge, Frenchee offers this wisdom: "See a nutritionist and get a diet plan and stick with it, but set goals that are realistic for you. The diet listed vegetables like broccoli, but I don't eat that. I like green beans, which were also on the list, so I ate those. I didn't follow the model exactly but found what fit my lifestyle and preferences. The English muffins and peanut butter really worked for me." Frenchee's friends and family, impressed by his achievements, jumped on the bandwagon. "Friends and people at work asked how I did it, so I gave them copies of the diet," he says. "My sister tried it and lost eighty pounds. Is there a size 2? I think she's a size 4 or 2 now, down from a 14." Frenchee says that a lot of his motivation came from knowing that he just had to "do it."

Losing weight is one thing; keeping it off is another. He's put on a little weight and hovers around 140 pounds, but he pays attention to his weight and knows what to do when it creeps up—and at fifty-three years old still fits into those 32/33 jeans. "I'm not so crazy with it now," he says. "Like tonight, we're having takeout, so I'll probably have a calzone with cheese, but I don't do that every night anymore. Sometimes I have a Coke at work, but not every day. My girlfriend keeps after me. She'll tell me, 'You can't eat that fast food.' There are all kinds of crazy diets coming out every day, but I've figured out what works for me."

A Problem in Two Parts: High LDL and High Triglycerides

In Chapter 1, I talked about the main cholesterol problem that affects people: high LDL levels. Although the numbers vary according to age, gender, and ethnic background, about 5 percent to 10 percent of people with this problem are also plagued by another: high triglyceride levels. In these people, triglyceride levels are typically in the 300–600 range. In one landmark study of heart disease risk published more than thirty years ago, it was this combination lipid disorder that was the most commonly seen lipid abnormality in younger individuals who had experienced a heart attack. This combination lipid disorder is more dangerous than elevated triglyceride or LDL level alone.

In people with this duo of problems, poor lifestyle choices are often to blame. The same factors that raise the LDL or triglyceride level in isolation should be carefully reviewed in someone who has an elevation in both. With proper attention to those issues, it is possible to treat the whole lipid disorder without medication or to at least solve one of the problems, which makes therapy easier.

Sometimes, though, a genetic problem can cause VLDL particles, which normally turn to LDL particles as their triglycerides are extracted for energy use, to get stuck in the middle. Like VLDL particles, these intermediate-density lipoproteins (IDL) are high in triglycerides, but they also have a relatively high content of cholesterol. So individuals with this genetic problem appear to have a combined lipid disorder (too much VLDL and LDL), when in fact they have an abnormal accumulation of IDL.

If lifestyle therapies can't correct the problem, most people with a combination of high triglycerides and LDL cholesterol get started on a fibrate drug. Most of the time, they also need a statin to get their lipoproteins to desirable levels. (Some doctors prefer to reverse this order of drug use, starting with a statin and then adding a fibrate.) Though this combination of medications is very effective at getting both triglycerides and LDL levels under control, it can exacerbate the main side effect of statins—the muscle damage known as rhabdomyolysis that can lead to kidney failure and, very rarely, death.

In any case, you shouldn't let that potential problem stop you from taking this combination if your doctor recommends it—the risks of having high triglycerides combined with high LDL levels are too great. However, you should be aware of this possible side effect and be on the lookout for muscle aches, the first sign that there's a problem. The muscle aches feel similar to postworkout aches and generally affect the larger muscles of the body, like the buttocks, thighs, calves, and shoulders. They may progress to muscle weakness that stops you from normal activities like climbing stairs, or muscles that hurt when you touch or squeeze them.

If you feel any dull pain or achiness in your muscles that can't be explained by exercise you've done, stop taking the medications and call your doctor immediately. He or she will generally take you off the medications for a few days. If your muscle aches stop, you'll probably be prescribed a new statin with the same fibrate and told to be vigilantly on the lookout for muscle aches. When the muscle breakdown known as rhabdomyolysis is occurring, the body releases more of a protein called creatine kinase. Though there is a test for this protein, as I discuss on page 152, I don't think testing for it is generally very useful in deciding if lipid drugs are safe to use. The best way to do that is to be on the lookout for muscle aches. However, if you were to develop significant muscle breakdown as a result of statin-fibrate combination therapy, the CPK level would be elevated and is useful in helping your doctor decide the severity of the injury and what kind of treatment you need.

Many people with muscle aches caused by a single statin or a statin-fibrate combination find that the aches occur only with certain statins. In fact, this is what happened in my case. I was on a plane flying to a medical conference when I noticed an achiness in my hips that I couldn't attribute to anything. Because I was newly taking a statin at the time to control my rising cholesterol levels, I immediately thought about all the patients I had treated who had voiced a similar complaint. I stopped taking the drug, and the muscle aches stopped almost immediately. When I switched to a different statin, they never came back. For some people, though, all of the statins cause the same achiness. In these cases, the safest thing to do is to take a different cholesterol-lowering drug, such as ezetimibe or niacin. For individuals on combined therapy with a statin and a fibrate, it is perfectly reasonable to continue the fibrate and swap the statin for niacin or ezetimibe. Note, though, that these combinations usually reduce LDL levels much less than

Why Won't My Doctor Prescribe a Statin-Fibrate Combination?

Some primary care doctors are hesitant to prescribe this combination of drugs after the deaths and other problems caused when the no-longer-available statin Baycol was mixed with fibrates. There is also a warning in the labeling of all statin medications that generally advises that they not be used in combination with fibrate therapy. Lipid specialists know that despite the risks, a statin-fibrate combination is an extremely effective way to lower lipids when combined disorders are present. As long as a patient is fully educated to watch for serious muscle side effects, I believe this combination can be safely used. If a person were unable to recognize or communicate the presence of muscle pains for any reason, however, this combination treatment should probably not be used. If you have a combined lipid disorder but your doctor is shying away from statin-fibrate therapy, you might want to ask for a referral to someone in your community who specializes in the treatment of lipid disorders.

the statin-fibrate pair, which is why it's important to try several different statins first.

Tackling Blood Lipids from More than One Side

Mark Brown has spent thirty years combating high cholesterol. "Back then when my doctor found my high cholesterol there wasn't as much known about it. I was given a diet but not much else." When he switched doctors fifteen years later, his new physician was concerned—and there were now more medical therapies to offer. Mark tried several medications, but none of them did much. "The levels fluctuated a little, but basically, it was a waste of time."

Yet a third doctor thought a referral to a gastroenterologist might be a good idea. Mark learned he had a condition in which there is a buildup of fat in the liver cells. This was a bit of a clue to the underlying problem. High triglyceride levels can contribute to fatty liver disease. Several additional attempts to lower his cholesterol with medication yielded disappointing results.

When I met Mark, it was clear that in order to bring his cholesterol down, we needed to attack the triglyceride problem. We started with the fibrate drug Tricor, which works by blocking VLDL production in the liver and by triggering the triglyceride-removal process. But ratcheting up the triglyceride-removal process in a patient with very high triglycerides also speeds up the conversion of VLDL to LDL. That means taking a fibrate alone will not only lower triglycerides but will also increase LDL levels. That's why these patients often need a fibrate and a statin (combination therapy). The first statin we tried wasn't a great success. "I had every annoying side effect listed," says Mark. "I experienced hair loss, gained weight, and had muscle cramps and spasms and excessive sweating." Cutting the dose didn't help, so we tried Lescol, which has worked well for him with few side effects. As it turns out, Mark's triglyceride and cholesterol troubles responded well to a one-two pharmaceutical punch. Combined therapy dramatically improved his lipid profile.

But his newfound passion for cycling helped too. "When we're in Florida, I'll bike as many as 150 to 200 miles per week. In Massachusetts the weather isn't as conducive to exercising outdoors—and I work more—so I'll get in maybe 70 to 100 miles. My wife rides too, and we joined a bike club in Florida." Most of us know how difficult it can be to find and stick with an exercise program. "Find an activity you love to do," advises Mark. When asked about the appeal of cycling, he describes the feeling of covering a good amount of distance at a pretty fast clip. He also enjoys being outside and has lengthy bike routes in both states that go along the water. He and his wife have even started kayaking. Apart from an improved lipid profile, Mark gets other benefits from exercise. "On days I don't exercise, I really feel it. It helps with my stress and also gives me more energy. When I don't ride or work out, I'm ready for bed by 9:00. When I do exercise I'm raring to go until 11:00. I know it seems like it shouldn't be that way, but it is." Mark says he knows diet is important, but he isn't as vigilant as he might be. "Controlling my carb intake does help with the triglycerides, but it can make cycling hard, so days I know I'll be riding I do eat more carbohydrates. I know that diet is important, but I also want to still enjoy life, including food."

Thirty years is a long time to struggle with high cholesterol. When asked what kept him working on it, Mark explains, "I knew I had to do something. At age fifty-two I had already lost younger friends to heart disease and cancer." He credits much of his success to working with the right specialist. "If you have a serious issue, find someone who knows that issue really well. If you have trouble with your car's air conditioner you can go to a gas station, Firestone, Sears. But there's no guarantee that they'll find what's wrong and fix it. You want to go to an air-conditioning specialist who works on your brand of car," Mark says. As with many patients, it took a bit of trial and error to find the right statin for Mark. "When you watch the TV ads it seems like everyone should be on one drug. If you try one and things don't improve, you really need to find out why and consider a switch," he says.

Low HDL

Recommendations for people with low HDL levels are a little less cut-and-dried than those for the other lipid problems. That's because we don't have any studies showing specifically that if we raise HDL levels, heart disease risk goes down. We know HDL is good for the heart, so we believe that the higher the levels the better, but no studies have unequivocally proved that. Why? Because all the drugs we employ to raise HDL levels typically lower the LDL or triglyceride values at the same time. This makes it hard to tell which change caused the benefit of fewer heart problems. Recent animal studies have also shown that there may be good ways to raise an HDL cholesterol level and bad ways to do that, so without knowing how a drug has led to a change in HDL, one can't readily predict if its effects would be beneficial or detrimental.

How High Is High Enough for HDL?

NCEP guidelines are as follows:

Less than 40 mg/dL	Low (causing increased risk)
60 mg/dL and above	High (heart-protective)

None of the statins alter HDL levels very dramatically (about 4 percent to 10 percent increase), whereas the fibrates and niacin do a better job of raising HDL levels (about 10 percent to 15 percent). Despite the unanswered questions about treating HDL, it is a very important blood value, with some studies indicating it predicts coronary disease risk better than any other single lipid value. The large observational study called the Framingham Heart Study suggests that every 1 mg/dL decrease in HDL increased the risk of having a heart attack by 2 percent to 3 percent. And the NCEP classifies an HDL level below 40 as a major risk factor for developing heart disease.

Most doctors don't often prescribe medications to raise HDL levels, because the drug that works best—niacin—can be hard to take and may have side effects that are particularly undesirable in the population most likely to have low HDL levels: diabetics. More options should become available in the near future, as the study of HDL metabolism is the most active area of cutting-edge research in the lipid field, and several new approaches are currently in early clinical trials. Luckily, though, there are a lot of lifestyle changes that raise HDL levels that are also beneficial to the rest of your cholesterol profile, your heart in general, and just about every other part of your body. The following can help you raise your HDL level:

- Exercising
- Not smoking
- Avoiding foods with trans fats (a lot of margarines, fried foods, some commercial baked goods)

- Losing weight if you're overweight
- Drinking a small amount of alcohol every day (typically one drink for women, two for men)

Again, while we don't know if raising HDL through these changes will help prevent heart disease, we do know that their other benefits will definitely decrease heart disease risk.

CHAPTER 10

Special Considerations for Seniors, Children, and People with Heart Disease or Diabetes

As I've said throughout the book, the best way to get the care you need is to talk to your doctor so you can take your individual needs and characteristics into account when deciding what to do. This book and general recommendations like those of the NCEP are only guidelines. This is especially true for people who fall into the following categories. If you're one of them, remember that the general things you read about cholesterol treatments might not apply to you.

If You're a Senior

It's especially important for seniors with high cholesterol to get treatment. Risk for heart attack increases with age, so taking care to manage other risk factors—including high cholesterol—has a large impact on this age group's health.

Many things about lowering cholesterol, including cutoffs for healthy and unhealthy cholesterol levels, are the same for seniors as for younger adults. But some things are slightly different. For example, some studies point out that low HDL is a particularly potent risk factor in this group. A study on close to four thousand older people from the National Institutes of Health, for example, found that people with HDL levels below 35 were two and a half times more likely to die of heart disease during the six-year study than people with higher HDL levels. Other studies have shown that total cholesterol levels don't correspond with heart disease as strongly in older people as they do in younger people. This might be explained by a simple fact of life: the older you are, the more likely you are to die of another cause before cholesterol has a chance to wreak havoc on your heart.

The issue of treating seniors is complex and controversial. Much of the controversy can be attributed to a certain ambivalence in society, shared by some physicians, about the value of introducing preventive medicine therapies to people who have already reached or surpassed their natural life expectancy.

Before there were studies in older individuals, it was frequently stated that the side effect profile would be worse or the effectiveness of the drugs would be lower than in younger people, so it wasn't good medicine to give statins to seniors. Now, with several studies in hand, these arguments can largely be dismissed. The 2004 NCEP guidelines point to several new studies that show the benefits of treating seniors, including the Prospective Study of Pravastatin in the Elderly at Risk. This study included only individuals ranging in age from seventy to eighty-two. Within three years, substantially fewer of those taking pravastatin (Pravachol) had a heart attack or stroke, or died from one. This and other studies in seniors showed that they tolerated the statin medicines quite well and the benefits appear to be every bit as good as those seen in younger age groups.

That said, many seniors have other medical problems that can make treating cholesterol more complicated because of drug interactions or organ damage that affects the metabolism of the drugs. Often, elderly patients can be effectively treated with lower doses of medication because of slower drug-clearance times or decreased body mass. These, however, are not reasons to avoid treatment with statins. The treatment just may need to be individualized.

None of these issues, however, address the philosophical question of whether we should spend our health-care dollars to treat elderly individuals in order to prevent future disease. Because our health-care system does not ration care based on age, I think the answer to this question can be provided only when a patient sits down with his or her doctor and discusses the specific pros and cons of this decision in the context of that patient's health and personal philosophy. In general, the better the health and life expectancy of an older person, the more it makes sense to work to prevent coronary artery disease and stroke, the major killers of the elderly. If an older person is already known to have coronary disease or a high stroke risk, lipid-lowering therapy should be used in most circumstances unless a specific medical problem stands in the way.

Issues That Arise for Seniors

For some seniors, obtaining or preparing a heart-healthy diet is difficult. Once you've read Chapter 6 and know what constitutes a healthy diet, you're halfway there. But if the other half—putting the knowledge into action—seems undoable, ask for help. Your local agency on aging probably has lists of services for seniors, including people who can do your food shopping or deliver premade meals. Religious organizations, senior centers, and some community groups may also offer free or low-cost meals. If you can do your own shopping but prefer not to cook, there is a wide variety of healthy prepared meals in the freezer or deli sections of most supermarkets.

For seniors who are prescribed a medication to keep cholesterol down, this addition to what may already be a large arsenal of pills can be expensive or inconvenient. There are a few solutions to these problems. Information in Chapter 8 lists many ways to save money on drugs. There are also quite a few ways to manage the other aspects of taking multiple medications. These are some of my favorites:

- **Get a buddy**. If you (or someone you care for) take more than three medications, have memory problems, or have a history of not complying with a drug regimen, you should find someone who can help you. This person can double-check that you're following your doctor's directions, help you if you have trouble opening packages or reading their fine print, and call your doctor if there's a problem. Usually a spouse or child fills this role, but neighbors, clergypeople, or friends can also help. This person doesn't need any sort of medical training, but he or she might want to talk to your doctor to get information on your medication regimen.

- **Make a drug chart.** In Chapter 8 (Figure 8.2), you'll find a drug chart that you can either photocopy or write on directly. It'll help you keep track of what medications you take, why, when, at what dose, for how long, anything you need to avoid while on the medication, and major side effects and what to do if they occur. Don't forget to include any herbal supplements or vitamins. Bring the chart to appointments with your doctors or to the pharmacy so someone can look it over to make sure you're taking your medications correctly and that none of them interact with one another.

- **Buy an organizer.** Many drugstores sell pill organizers that have labeled compartments (for example, marked "Lunch" or "Bedtime") that can help remind you to take your medications at the right time, as well as calibrated spoons or syringes to help you dispense the correct dose of liquid medicines. If you need a stronger reminder, you may want to buy containers that beep or blink when it's time to take a medication. Some containers have a cap that counts how many times a bottle has been opened to help tally daily doses. Check with your pharmacist to be sure that the dispenser you prefer won't compromise the strength of your medicines by exposing them to moisture, light, or oxygen.

• **Talk to your doctor.** A lot of older people have trouble swallowing pills. If you're one of them, your doctor may be able to prescribe pills in smaller forms or show you how to crush pills and mix them with a drink if appropriate.

If Your Child Has High Cholesterol

Like a lot of problems adults face, high cholesterol may start in childhood and progress into adulthood. Eating and exercise habits also carry over from younger years. This means it's especially important for kids to eat right, exercise, and not smoke.

Most people don't need to get a fasting lipid profile until they hit twenty. However, the Committee on Nutrition of the American Academy of Pediatrics recommends checking the cholesterol levels of children older than two who have risk factors like a family history of early heart disease or high cholesterol. The committee recommends that doctors and parents talk about screening kids and teens who are obese, are inactive, smoke, have high blood pressure, or have diabetes. Although it's important for adults to have repeat cholesterol tests if levels are found to be high, this is even more important in children, whose levels can vary more than adults'. Table 10.1 gives the cholesterol guidelines for children.

Treating Children

Children are not just "miniature adults," so their treatment for most conditions is different. In the case of borderline or high cho-

TABLE 10.1 Cholesterol Guidelines for Children

	Total Cholesterol (mg/dL)	LDL Cholesterol (mg/dL)
Acceptable	<170	<110
Borderline	170–199	110–129
High	≥200	≥130

Reprinted with permission from American Academy of Pediatrics Committee on Nutrition, "Cholesterol in Childhood," *Pediatrics*, 101 (1), page 145.

lesterol, the American Academy of Pediatrics recommends a two-step diet approach first. Only when those steps don't work will medication be considered, and then only in children older than ten. The safety of cholesterol medications just hasn't been tested in younger children. In kids older than ten, the American Academy of Pediatrics recommends using only the drugs that are not absorbed into the bloodstream but that work by blocking cholesterol absorption in the intestine (e.g., the bile acid resins cholestyramine and colestipol).

Children with extremely high cholesterol levels (usually due to a genetic disorder) may need medication in order to prevent a heart attack at a very early age. A 2004 study that randomly assigned children with familial hypercholesterolemia to either pravastatin or a placebo found that the statin was effective and caused no side effects in children during the two years of the study.

Personally, I try to avoid treating children with cholesterol medications. I feel treatment can usually wait because heart attacks are incredibly rare in males or females under the age of thirty. (When they do occur, there is almost always a very strong genetic predisposition to heart disease. In these cases, the young person's lipid profile is typically very abnormal and needs to be treated.) Lipid therapies take only a few years, at the longest, to confer benefits, so I believe children don't need to go on medication in all but the most severe cases. While many thoughtful physicians might disagree with this opinion, arguing instead that it is better to intervene against the development of atherosclerosis as soon as possible, I don't believe this view is backed by enough evidence to adopt it in clinical practice at this time. A 2004 study brought good news for those children who do need medication: researchers who treated kids with familial hypercholesterolemia with either a statin or a placebo found that the statin was effective and caused no side effects.

As in adults, cholesterol is just one of many risk factors for heart disease. Children should also keep their blood pressure in control, not smoke, watch for and treat diabetes, keep weight at healthy levels, and keep active.

TABLE 10.2 Diets for Children Older than Two with Borderline or High Cholesterol

Step 1	Step 2
Daily fat intake between 20 percent and 30 percent of total calories	Detailed assessment of eating habits
10 percent or less of daily calories from polyunsaturated fats	Same daily fat and polyunsaturated fat goals as in Step 1
Less than 10 percent of daily calories from saturated fats	Less than 7 percent of calories from saturated fat
300 mg or less of cholesterol per day	200 mg or less of cholesterol per day
Diet monitored by clinician	Careful planning (often with the help of a dietitian) to ensure the child on this diet gets adequate vitamins and minerals

Source: Adapted from American Academy of Pediatrics Committee on Nutrition, "Cholesterol in Childhood," *Pediatrics*, 101 (1), pages 141–147.

Preventing High Cholesterol in Children

Prevention is always the best medicine, and this is definitely the case for heart disease in children. Atherosclerosis or its precursors begin in childhood, and high cholesterol during this time may play a role in causing adult atherosclerosis. If your children don't have high cholesterol, it's still a great time to get them started with a healthy lifestyle. Encourage them to exercise and eat right. Children under two should not be on fat-restrictive diets, but after that, adopting the Step 1 diet (see Table 10.2) is a good way for children and adolescents to prevent heart disease. And best of all, doing so usually means that you have to adopt these healthy habits, too.

If You Have Heart Disease

A lot of my patients wonder about the point of lowering cholesterol after a heart attack or other sign of heart disease. "Isn't it a waste of time?" they ask. The answer is an emphatic NO. Once you've had a heart attack, you're at a much greater risk of having another. Because the risk is higher, the treatment benefits are even greater. This statement isn't my medical opinion; it is one of the best-studied issues in all of medicine. The 1994 4S trial discussed earlier was the first to document the benefit of lowering cholesterol in patients who had preexisting heart disease, but even as recently as 2004, the PROVE-IT trial showed the benefit of lowering LDL to under 65 mg/dL in individuals with recent heart attack symptoms. (This was one of the studies that led the NCEP to add 70 mg/dL as an optional goal LDL level for people with heart disease.) In the decade that separated those two reports, many other studies that used a variety of statins have showed a benefit on either mortality or a new coronary event in patients with preexisting heart disease. So, if you have already had a heart attack, you should be even more aggressive about treating any lipid or other risk factor you have that would make it more likely for you to experience the same problem again.

If You Have Diabetes

The fight for a healthy heart is even more important for people with diabetes than it is for people without. According to the American Diabetes Association, over a ten-year period, people with diabetes have a 15 percent to 25 percent chance of developing heart problems, and more than 65 percent of people with diabetes die from heart disease or stroke.

Experts don't fully understand why diabetes causes cardiovascular disease, but it's clear that people with diabetes—especially type 2 diabetes—often have various heart disease risk factors, such as high cholesterol, high blood pressure, high triglycerides, and obesity. Diabetes also tips the balance of good and bad cholesterols in an unhealthy direction. Most diabetics have low HDL and high triglyceride levels and many have LDL levels above the current 100 mg/dL target goal. The high blood sugar associated with diabetes may have another negative affect on cholesterol—it may be responsible for accelerating the chemical change known as oxidation of LDL cholesterol. Many scientists suspect that oxidized LDL cholesterol plays a key role in initiating the inflammatory damage that causes atherosclerosis.

It's especially important for people with diabetes to limit their intake of foods with high cholesterol or saturated fat content.

Differences Between the Sexes on Cholesterol?

For a long time, medical studies didn't include women because researchers were afraid that their menstrual cycle would skew results or that the subjects would become pregnant and have to stop taking a medication. Younger women were also less likely to have heart disease, which meant more participants would have to be included to be able to show a difference in outcomes if women were involved. More study subjects means more money to do the study, so leaving women out was a practical decision that wasn't as sexist as it sometimes appears.

Fortunately, once the benefit of a particular therapy was shown in men, the economics made it favorable to study women as well, and later studies have shown that women benefit just as much as men do from cholesterol-lowering interventions, whenever the risk is equivalent. By the time women are in their midsixties, their risk of new coronary events is similar to that of similarly aged men, so there should be little difference in treatment at that point. In younger, premenopausal women, the risk for heart disease is less than that of men, so fewer women in this age group require treatment. However, when all risk factors are taken into account, men and women of equivalent risk for heart disease get treated to the same LDL target goals.

However, even if you follow a strict diet and exercise program, it's likely that you won't be able to get your cholesterol under control without medication. Don't think this is a free pass to pop a pill and ignore your diet, however—it's especially important for people with diabetes to pull out all the stops in terms of cholesterol control.

The 2004 NCEP guidelines stress the importance of controlling cholesterol if you have diabetes. The panel notes it is reasonable for people with both diabetes and heart disease to strive for the very low LDL level of 70 mg/dL. For people with diabetes who don't have a heart condition, the panel suggests an LDL goal of 100, with the option to push levels even lower. However, the NCEP also notes that not everyone with diabetes needs a cholesterol-lowering drug. If a person with diabetes is young and has no other risk factors, he or she has moderate risk of heart disease and can implement lifestyle changes as long as LDL levels stay below 130 mg/dL. If they go higher, drug therapy can be used.

On the Horizon

Medicine changes fast, and if you've been following news on heart health in the past few years, you'll know that cholesterol treatment is no exception. New studies are constantly leading to a new understanding of how best to combat cholesterol's ill effects on the heart. I'm sure that as time goes on, that understanding will only deepen. While I can't predict what future studies will find, I can tell you that there are a few treatments and questions that are under study right now whose results look promising.

Increasing HDL Levels

The PROVE IT study discussed earlier in the book brought up another point besides the possible benefit of lowering LDL levels to below 100. In this trial, among the people in the aggressive treatment group who lowered their LDLs a lot, 22.4 percent had a coronary event. That means that although LDL lowering is an important part of therapy, even if you have low LDL levels, you're not completely safe. The logical next addition to your heart-protection program is something to increase your HDL. Even though increasing HDL hasn't been proved to decrease the risk of heart problems, I'm fairly confident that it does. The issues are really which is the best way to raise an HDL level and whether there are some ways that confer a benefit and others that don't.

197

Besides the more established methods mentioned earlier in this book, there are a few things on the horizon for HDL, including the following.

CETP

It's long been known that a protein called cholesterol ester transfer protein (CETP) plays a key role in determining HDL cholesterol levels. CETP helps exchange cholesterol between lipoproteins and can transfer it from HDL to the lower-density lipoproteins, LDL and VLDL. Individuals with a genetic mutation that causes loss of all CETP activity have very high levels of HDL cholesterol. They appear to be at lower risk of coronary disease. A small study in 2004 looked at whether a drug called torcetrapib, which blocks CETP from working, increases HDL cholesterol levels. The researchers gave two different doses of torcetrapib to nineteen people with low HDL, about half of whom were also treated with a statin for their high LDL. HDL levels doubled in the group given the highest dose of torcetrapib without the statin. These are very large increases in HDL levels, much higher than we can achieve with existing lipid drugs.

Of course, though this points researchers in a promising direction, therapy with torcetrapib is not ready for prime time. It needs to be tested in a larger population, and it needs to be proved that treatment with it doesn't only increase HDL levels but also prevents heart problems. It will likely take three to four years before the effect on heart problems is clearly known, but the development of an effective and safe HDL-raising drug could be as important in the prevention of heart disease as was the development of statins.

HDL-Infusion Therapy

A group of forty people in a small Italian village led to the discovery of a rare type of HDL that seemed to protect against heart disease even when the levels of HDL were not very high. How could that be? They had a protein in their HDL, now called ApoA-I Milano, that seemed to be better at stimulating the removal of cholesterol from plaques than was HDL containing the normal protein, called apo A-I. (You may remember news reports on ApoA-I Milano calling it "Drano for the heart.")

Researchers recently tested whether a synthetic version of ApoA-I Milano infused into the blood of people who didn't have this protein naturally would have the same effect. The small trial randomly assigned forty-seven people who had recently had heart attacks to receive either a placebo or a low or high dose of this chemical. Through ultrasounds of the arteries, researchers found that from the beginning to the end of the five-week trial, the plaque in the treatment groups shrank by 4 percent, while that of the placebo group increased by a small amount.

Though these are exciting results, bear in mind that this one small trial doesn't prove that infusions of this supercharged HDL will help prevent heart disease or that it will even decrease plaque in a larger population of patients. But it does look promising. The small company that developed this treatment was recently acquired by a very large pharmaceutical company, so it is likely that much bigger trials of this approach will be started soon. Though FDA approval of this treatment may still be several years away, it is probable that patients with heart disease who have low HDL levels could receive this treatment in a clinical trial much sooner.

High-Tech Scans

Right now, the best way to "see" your heart's arteries and determine if or how badly they're clogged is to snake a catheter in through an artery in the leg or arm and get an angiogram, as discussed in Chapter 3. A less invasive procedure that's just as accurate would be ideal, and researchers are trying to find one. Some noninvasive screening tests are on the market already, but they aren't covered by insurance—and they run in the thousands of

Should I Participate in a Clinical Trial?

In the best clinical trials, there are patients who receive treatment and those who receive a placebo. So if you sign up to participate in a clinical trial that has a placebo arm, you could get this fake treatment instead of the real one. You should also remember that the active treatment arm in a study may be found not to work or to have some previously unknown side effects, so getting randomized to the placebo arm of a trial should not be viewed as losing out. Despite these possible drawbacks, I would still encourage participation in these kinds of studies because they enable us to more quickly determine if a drug works and get approval for everyone to use it if it does. By participating in a study, you are advancing the development of medical science in a way that may very well benefit you or someone you love.

dollars. Advertisements and features on popular shows like "Oprah" are provoking some people to get them anyway. Should you? Probably not, but here is some more information on why I'm skeptical about their use and what needs to be proved to make them more usable in the mainstream population.

CT Scans

Computed tomography machines (usually called CT or CAT scanners) take x-ray pictures of thin "slices" of your anatomy, and then a computer assembles these images into a three-dimensional picture. A jazzed-up version of the CT scanner, called electron beam computed tomography (EBCT) or ultrafast CT, is fast enough to capture a still picture of the beating heart.

The EBCT can precisely measure how much calcium is in the heart's arteries. This is useful because normal arteries usually don't contain calcium, while arteries chock-full of it are often clogged with atherosclerotic plaque. The constant cycle of damage and repair that leads to atherosclerosis also shrouds the artery walls with crusty calcium deposits. As a general rule, the more extensive the calcium deposits, the more extensive the atherosclerosis.

However, a high or low calcium score doesn't actually prove anything. Results from studies of EBCT scans and cardiovascular risk are all over the map. *In general*, they suggest that a low calcium score indicates little atherosclerosis and a low risk for heart attack or other cardiovascular event over the next two to five years, and a high calcium score suggests plenty of atherosclerosis and a higher-than-average risk. But many people at risk for coronary disease have calcium scores somewhere in the middle, and this is where the controversy really heats up.

A test used to detect a silent disease like atherosclerosis should meet several conditions. It shouldn't indicate that a disease is present when it really isn't (a false-positive result) or that it isn't present when it really is (a false-negative result). And a new test should also be better, or at least cheaper, than existing ones. As things stand now, ultrafast CT scans don't quite meet these standards. When it comes to predicting the chance of having a heart attack or dying from heart disease, these scans are about as good as taking the free, two-minute Framingham risk score that many doctors use to estimate heart disease risk.

What's more, a positive scan usually generates other tests and procedures, often including cardiac catheterization with coronary angiography to see if one or more coronary arteries is narrowed or blocked. About 40 percent of the time, the angiogram offers reassuring news, showing no blockage. Unfortunately, it can cause an infection, punctured blood vessel, heart attack, or stroke. And some people with slightly narrowed arteries that weren't causing any symptoms—and that may never have led to heart disease—end up with an angioplasty or even bypass surgery, which have low but definite risks for heart attack, stroke, and even death.

A large, multicenter study funded by the National Heart, Lung, and Blood Institute should tell us whether coronary artery

Dietary Calcium and the Heart

If calcium accumulating in the heart's arteries is a possible sign of impending heart disease, should you cut back on calcium in your diet or stop taking calcium supplements? No. Calcification happens whether you get a lot of calcium or a little.

In fact, there's mounting evidence that a diet rich in calcium from low-fat dairy products, fruits, and vegetables can actually protect you from high blood pressure and possibly from heart disease itself.

calcium scores are a good way to estimate the chances of having a heart attack. This study, called the Multi-Ethnic Study of Atherosclerosis, will test whether EBCT and other technologies effectively detect hidden cardiovascular disease among more than fourteen thousand volunteers. Although the study is designed to last up to ten years, it could yield an answer sooner.

Until then, I recommend that you save your money. But if you decide to have an EBCT, talk it over with your cardiologist or another trusted doctor. He or she can help you put your risk for heart disease—and maybe the benefits and risks of this test—in perspective.

MRI for the Heart

Taking a clear picture of coronary arteries from outside the body is not an easy task. These blood vessels are as narrow as spaghetti, and they weave over the heart's surface, intertwining with coronary veins and bouncing around with every breath and heartbeat. But a magnetic resonance imaging (MRI) technique developed by Harvard Medical School researchers yields images clear enough to detect narrowed or blocked arteries.

Doctors in the United States and Europe tested this MRI scan on 109 men and women right before they underwent coronary angiography. The scan spotted 72 percent of the diseased arteries identified by the angiograms. Though the results are impressive, further study and fine-tuning of this noninvasive screening method is needed to have it pass the ultimate hurdle of becoming faster, safer, more accurate, and less expensive than angiography.

Other Scans

These scans won't be available until sometime in the future, if they become available to the mainstream public at all:

- **Ultrasound.** Sound waves bounce off the squishy, fat-filled center of vulnerable plaque in different ways than they bounce off fibrous plaque or healthy artery walls. Blasting blood vessels with sound waves and recording how they are absorbed and reflected lets doctors map healthy and diseased sections of artery.
- **Optical coherence tomography.** This is like ultrasound, only using light from a tiny source similar to the one used in a compact disc player.
- **Thermography.** Vulnerable plaque tends to be a hot spot—literally—of inflammation. By recording the heat radiated from different sections of artery wall, tiny sensors gently drawn through an artery could pinpoint vulnerable plaque.
- **Near-infrared spectroscopy.** The same technology used to identify rocks on Mars is being focused on heart disease. Because vulnerable plaque has a different chemical composition than stable plaque or healthy artery walls, it absorbs and reflects light with a unique light "signature."

Over-the-Counter Statins

In 2004, the United Kingdom approved statins for sale over the counter. Many people began to ask if this would happen in the United States as well. Indeed, drug companies are already working on making this a possibility. I, for one, hope they do not succeed.

Over-the-counter drugs are great for medical problems like a cold or headache. These are problems that a person can immediately identify—and he or she can tell when they're going away. If, for example, you take a cold medicine for a runny nose and sore throat, you know that when the symptoms abate, your cold is getting better. Your results and side effects don't need to be monitored by a doctor. The same cannot be said for treating high cholesterol. First, you need a lab test to diagnose it. And, more important, you need continued lab tests to determine if your treatment is working. So if your doctor told you that you had high cholesterol and you treated yourself with an over-the-counter statin, an important part of the process would be missing: You wouldn't know whether or not the treatment was working. Were your LDL levels dropping low enough? Were your triglyceride levels safe? What about HDL? Doctors have better control over monitoring patients' results on prescription medications because they can set a schedule for visits linked to refilling the prescription. This monitoring is the only way you and your doctor can know whether you need more help making lifestyle changes or another drug to better control different aspects of your cholesterol. The notion that statins should be available over the counter is a misunderstanding of how complex a problem high cholesterol is.

Another problem with over-the-counter statins is that if patients don't have to go to their doctors to get refills, they may never be asked about side effects. This lapse can be dangerous, especially if a patient doesn't link muscle aches to the statin and continues taking it. Also, pregnant women should not take statins—another thing that's easier to ensure when you need to see a doctor to get a prescription.

Because over-the-counter drugs are not covered by insurance, increasing out-of-pocket cost for the drug is another issue. At the same time, as patient cost goes up, the cost for the health-care system goes down. It is important to keep medical costs down in order to have a fiscally viable health-care system. However, in this case, drug companies would also reap the financial benefit because as the drugs lose their patents and generic versions are available without a prescription, going over the counter would boost the brand-name drugs' sales.

Genetics, Lipids, and Heart Disease

One of the most exciting advances in recent years was the sequencing of the human genome—the key to identifying the genes that make humans tick, and also get sick. Because this happened only a few years ago, the implications of this accomplishment are just beginning to be imagined. To understand what this scientific advance means to the human race, it is important to know where we were before it happened.

In the past three decades, medical science has devoted itself to the study of one gene at a time—genes that usually had profound impacts on a human disease. In the lipid field, researchers found a gene that, when mutated, could raise the blood LDL level close to 1,000 mg/dL. We also found a gene that caused the HDL cholesterol to plummet to 0 when mutated.

Medical scientists discovered these genes and others by studying the very rare people who had single gene mutations that caused profound alterations in their bodies. Diseases like cystic fibrosis and Huntington's disease are examples of disorders caused by the mutation of a single gene. A great deal of our understanding of normal human physiology has come from studying these rare individuals who had the misfortune to inherit mutations in one of these genes. Everyone in society has benefited from the willingness of those people to participate in studies of their condition, as these studies have led and will continue to lead to better therapies for those who have less serious forms of disease.

Most of us don't carry a major inactivating mutation in any of the genes that are responsible for leading a healthy life. What we do carry, however, are minor variations in these genes that, when combined with minor variations in other related genes, predispose us to developing chronic diseases as we age. Atherosclerotic heart disease is a prime example of the kind of disease that is most commonly produced by small changes in multiple genes rather than a big change in only one gene. The influence of genes on disease is also affected by environmental factors, making the prediction of disease outcome even more challenging. What the human genome sequence gives us is a road map of all the genes, and we are just now beginning to explore how a minor variation in several of them can ultimately lead to heart disease.

This information is likely to improve our ability to predict coronary disease risk much more accurately than we can today, and it may well help us target our therapies more specifically, based on gene function. Finally, there may even be genetically based therapies that can correct genetic abnormalities directly in a way that has never been possible before.

None of what I just outlined is going to happen at your next doctor's visit, but neither is it science fiction. A study in 1999 showed that mice who were engineered to have the same defect that humans with very high cholesterol levels have could be cured of this problem by injection of the appropriate gene. We can't yet routinely safely deliver and express genes in humans, but we now know that were it possible to do that, we could cure that specific cholesterol disorder. Many labs around the world are working on developing methods for safe gene delivery, and although that work has experienced some highly public failures and controversies, its ultimate success is likely to improve the lives of thousands of unfortunate people who had the bad luck to inherit a devastating genetic mutation.

Another exciting possibility that the human genome project has revealed is the potential for genetic information to better predict optimal treatments for medical conditions, including high cholesterol levels. A study published in the *Journal of the American Medical Association* in the summer of 2004 announced that small genetic variations from person to person create a considerable difference in how an individual responds to statin therapy. Genetic variation may be routinely measured someday and that information used by your physician to tailor a specific treatment regimen to your physiology.

Progress Takes Time

The advancements I have described in this chapter are not going to happen immediately. It will take time and a lot of hard work for them to be brought to a doctor's office or hospital near you. Academic medical centers, like the one in which I work, train and employ creative scientists and physicians who will be responsible for turning the basic science discoveries of the human genome sequence into improved medical care in the coming century. Your tax dollars and philanthropic support of those institutions make that possible, and all of us who work in these centers recognize our responsibility in making those advances occur as quickly as possible.

Alternative and Complementary Approaches to Lowering Cholesterol

A lot of my patients ask about alternative therapies they've heard about through friends or advertisements. Most of these remedies haven't been tested in a scientifically sound way to prove they benefit your cholesterol profile or lower heart disease risk. Does that mean they don't? No, but it also doesn't mean they do. My basic philosophy is that as long as the substance isn't dangerous, there's no harm in trying it out and seeing if it works for you. That said, even the most benign substance can be harmful in two situations:

1. If you stop taking your prescribed medicine or living a healthy lifestyle in hopes that the alternative treatment will replace them.
2. If you can't afford to be spending money on treatments that may or may not work. Some of my patients who have limited incomes spend money on alternative treatments that they hear will benefit their health. I often think this money

could be put to much better use in their lives. If you don't have much money to spare for your health-care needs, I'd suggest spending it on what's known to work rather than on products that sell on the basis of unscientific and unproven testimonials. What works for lipid lowering is what I have discussed in the previous chapters—diet, exercise, and the medications mentioned.

If you do an Internet search for alternative medicine and cholesterol, you'll get hundreds of thousands of websites that advertise all sorts of products. I obviously can't go into all of them in this chapter, but I will talk about the alternative therapies that are most often on my patients' minds. Where there is scientific evidence that supports their use, I'll share it, and where there is none, I'll tell you that, too. Refer also to Table 12.1.

TABLE 12.1 How Some Common Herbal Remedies May Affect the Heart

Herb	Possible CV Benefit	Possible CV Harm	Possible CV Drug Interactions
Danshen	May improve angina symptoms and survival after a heart attack	Platelet problems; constricts coronary arteries at high doses	May cause bleeding problems with warfarin, aspirin, or other antiplatelet drugs
Dong quai	May prevent clots; trial in stroke patients showed no benefit	Increased bleeding tendency	May cause bleeding problems with warfarin, aspirin, or other antiplatelet drugs
Echinacea (taken mainly to prevent infection)	None known	None known	May cause heart rhythm problems with amiodarone, cyclosporine, propafenone, or ibutilide; may interfere with immune-suppressing effects of cyclosporine

TABLE 12.1 How Some Common Herbal Remedies
May Affect the Heart, *continued*

Herb	Possible CV Benefit	Possible CV Harm	Possible CV Drug Interactions
Ephedra (ma huang)	None known	Stroke; heart attack; erratic rhythm; high blood pressure; sudden death	May interfere with drugs for heart rhythm irregularities or high blood pressure
Feverfew (taken mainly for migraine)	None known	Platelet problems	May cause bleeding problems with warfarin, aspirin, or other antiplatelet drugs
Garlic	May reduce cholesterol levels 5 percent to 15 percent; may lower blood pressure	Increased bleeding tendency	May cause bleeding problems with warfarin, aspirin, or other antiplatelet drugs
Ginger (taken mainly for nausea or dizziness)	None known	Platelet problems; high blood pressure	May cause bleeding problems with warfarin, aspirin, or other antiplatelet drugs
Ginkgo	May improve symptoms of claudication; may improve brain function after stroke or with low blood flow to the brain	Increased bleeding tendency; hemorrhagic stroke	May cause bleeding problems with warfarin, aspirin, or other antiplatelet drugs
Ginseng	May improve heart function in people with heart failure; possible small reduction in high blood pressure	High blood pressure with overuse	May cause bleeding problems with warfarin, aspirin, or other antiplatelet drugs
Guggul	May lower cholesterol	None known	None known
Hawthorn	May improve symptoms in people with heart failure; possible small reduction in cholesterol	None known	May interfere with digoxin

continued

TABLE 12.1 How Some Common Herbal Remedies May Affect the Heart, *continued*

Herb	Possible CV Benefit	Possible CV Harm	Possible CV Drug Interactions
Hellebore	May lower blood pressure	Low blood pressure; slow heart rate	None known
Horse chestnut seed extract	For chronic venous insufficiency, reduces swelling in legs and feet about as much as compression stockings	None known	None known
Kava	None known	Platelet problems	May cause bleeding problems with warfarin, aspirin, or other antiplatelet drugs
Saint-John's-wort (usually taken for depression)	None known	Possible high blood pressure	May interfere with digoxin, calcium channel blockers, quinidine, amiodarone, and cyclosporine
Saw palmetto (usually taken for prostate enlargement)	None known	None known	None known
Yohimbine	May improve sudden drops in blood pressure upon standing	High blood pressure; heart rhythm problems	May interfere with drugs for high blood pressure and heart rhythm abnormalities

Source: "Herbs and the Heart," *Harvard Heart Letter*, July 2002, page 3.

Coenzyme Q10

It seems logical that the antioxidant marketed as coenzyme Q10 (known medically as ubiquinone) would help prevent the muscle problems that statins can cause. It's been shown that when statins block the production of cholesterol, they also decrease the amount of ubiquinone the body creates. Plus, other muscle syndromes reduce levels of ubiquinone. So wouldn't raising ubiquinone levels through supplements decrease statins' effects on muscles?

Should You Trust Your Friends' and Family's Advice?

You hope that you can trust your friends and loved ones to tell you the truth about anything. So if one of them tells you about how this new herbal pill made the side effects of another drug completely disappear or lowered her cholesterol, why shouldn't you go out and get it? It might be a case of the placebo effect—where simply taking a pill plays a trick on the mind so the person thinks the symptoms are gone. That doesn't mean it will have the same effect on you, however. Or it might be that another change in your friend's life was truly behind the change in cholesterol, not the herbal treatment.

While the logic is there, the proof isn't. Very few studies have looked at ubiquinone in this light, and those that have were small and not entirely conclusive. One small study indicated that coenzyme Q10 might decrease the severity, if not the frequency, of muscle problems.

What does this mean to you? If a patient comes into my office and says that she's read or heard great things about coenzyme Q10, I would say that because statins decrease coenzyme Q10, there is a good theoretical reason to try this supplement, but I also tell her that with no large trials, there's no proof that it'll work.

Plant Sterols and Stanols

Plants make kinds of alcohols known as sterols and stanols for many of the same reasons that animals make cholesterol. They're key components of cell membranes, hormones, and some vitamins. Scientists have known since the early 1950s that sterols and stanols can lower cholesterol levels. In fact, these alcohols were components of an early generation of cholesterol-lowering medications. Then they faded from sight, replaced by ones that were easier to make, less unpleasant to take, and more effective. But

213

once Finnish researchers discovered in 1989 how to add the naturally insoluble sterols and stanols to a host of foods without changing their taste or texture, they began moving back to center stage in the fight against cholesterol. Foods enriched with plant sterols currently include juice, margarines, salad dressings, snack bars, and even chocolate.

An influential 1995 report in the *New England Journal of Medicine* described the results of a trial comparing a margarine that delivered about two grams of stanols a day with a stanol-free version of the same spread among more than 150 men and women with high cholesterol. After a year, those using the stanol-enriched spread had 14 percent lower LDL and 10 percent lower total cholesterol levels. Subsequent studies have demonstrated even larger reductions, in some cases equal to the effects of cholesterol-lowering drugs.

Overall, results from several trials suggest that eating two grams of plant sterols or stanols a day lowers LDL cholesterol levels by 9 percent to 20 percent. This may not sound like a lot, but it could make a big difference. Lowering your LDL level by 20 mg/dL (about what the average person can expect from eating a cholesterol-lowering spread *as part of a healthy diet*) and keeping it down could translate into a 25 percent lower risk of developing cardiovascular disease.

Adding phytosterols (a term encompassing the different types of plant sterols) to your diet is relatively easy. Eating more fruits, vegetables, and whole grains will give you small amounts of them. So will using vegetable oils like olive or canola oil. The most significant sources, though, are spreads such as Benecol or Take Control, or other foods enriched with plant sterols or stanols.

Because these products can't magically neutralize the cholesterol-raising effects of an unhealthy diet, they need to be part of an eating plan that's low in saturated and trans fats. To get a sustained cholesterol-lowering effect, you also need to eat enough to get two grams of phytosterols a day (about two servings of an enriched margarine). And you need to do this every day, just as you would take a cholesterol-lowering medication. Eating sterol- and stanol-enriched foods once in a while just won't work. Also, keep in mind that not everyone responds the same way to phytosterols. They lower cholesterol levels more in people who are genetically programmed to absorb lots of cholesterol from the intestines than they do in people who don't normally absorb much cholesterol.

Label readers will notice that regular Benecol and Take Control contain "partially hydrogenated vegetable oil," a phrase indicating the presence of the dreaded trans fats. Two servings a day adds about a gram of trans fats. That's not much all by itself. But so many foods contain trans fats that it's best to avoid them whenever possible. The "lite" versions of phytosterol-enriched margarines are free of trans fats.

In 2001, the American Heart Association recommended the use of stanol- and sterol-enriched foods only for adults with high total or LDL cholesterol, or those who have been diagnosed with cardiovascular disease. The Heart Association's cautious approach is justified, given that we don't have good information on the effects of long-term use, especially in children. The NCEP, however, encourages people with high cholesterol to use foods enriched with plant sterols and stanols (as well as high-fiber foods) as part of the lifestyle changes that lay the foundation for cholesterol-lowering strategies.

Could stanols and sterols also be good for people with normal or "high-normal" cholesterol levels? While there isn't evidence showing that phytosterols benefit such individuals, they just might. If you're worried about your cholesterol, these products are worth a try.

Foods enriched with plant sterols and stanols haven't been used long enough for researchers to establish their long-term effects. In the short term, they are safe for most people. But one group of people should stay away from these foods—those with the rare genetic disorder known as phytosterolemia or sitosterolemia, who absorb these substances at abnormally high rates. Once inside the body of people with this disorder, plant sterols and stanols accumulate and cause the same problems as too much cholesterol.

One possible side effect of eating plant sterols worries some nutrition experts. Plant sterols snare the fat-soluble vitamins A, E, D, K, and beta-carotene and keep them from being absorbed. In some studies, levels of these vitamins fell 10 percent to 25 percent among volunteers eating a phytosterol-enriched diet. Given the many important roles these nutrients play, chronically lowered levels *could* increase the chances of developing heart disease, cancer, or other diseases. Taking a standard multivitamin supplement may help counterbalance the loss of these nutrients. Another effect to think about is the impact on your wallet: spreads enriched with sterols and stanols cost much more than you'd pay for regular margarine.

Policosanol Alcohol

This dietary supplement made from alcohols extracted from sugarcane shows promise as a cholesterol-lowering agent. Though we're not sure exactly how it works, policosanol alcohol seems to block the production of cholesterol. Trials have shown it lowers LDL levels moderately in people with diabetes, postmenopausal women, the elderly, and those with familial hypercholesterolemia, the genetic disorder that causes high cholesterol. That said, most of the trials have been done by one group of scientists, and there haven't been as many long-term, independent clinical trials on policosanol alcohol as I would like to see before recommending it wholeheartedly. And more important, no one knows if policosanol's beneficial effects actually translate into lower incidents of heart attacks and strokes.

It does appear to be safe and not interact with most medications used to treat heart disease, though a trial focused on this question needs to be done. One noteworthy side effect is that it increases the effects of medications that decrease clotting (aspirin, warfarin). It probably should not be used with statins until the mechanism of action is better understood. Pregnant and breast-feeding women should also avoid it. Policosanol alcohol can decrease the stickiness of platelets, making you prone to bleed more than usual—especially if taken with aspirin.

Soy

As part of a healthy diet, soy can be a great substitute for red meat or other unhealthy foods. What's more controversial is whether or not soy should be taken as a supplement. Early studies suggested soy might lower LDL cholesterol, but more recent studies have cast doubt on this. So, for now, I don't recommend soy as anything other than a healthy protein source.

Red Yeast Rice

Though you might find red yeast rice (rice fermented by a kind of red yeast) on a menu in Asia, nowadays it's known mostly as a nutritional supplement. Studies show it lowering total cholesterol by 13 percent to 26 percent, LDL by 33 percent, and triglycerides by 13 percent to 34 percent. Some studies even show an increase in HDL cholesterol with its use.

Do these results sound too good to be true for a product you can buy without a prescription at a health food store? The FDA thought so. It banned the sale of red yeast rice in 2001. You see, red yeast rice works on cholesterol because it contains lovastatin, which is the same chemical compound as the statin Mevacor (and its generic counterpart). The FDA distinguishes between nutritional supplements, which are not regulated by the government, and drugs, which are. In this case, they decided red yeast rice should be monitored as a drug. However, the manufacturer won its case against the FDA, so it is available now. The problem is that products vary in amount and kind of statin they contain. It's unclear at this point whether red yeast rice offers any benefit over the prescribed statins. The chief advantage, in my opinion, is cost and the fact that you could buy this supplement without a prescription.

A few of my patients who've taken it experienced side effects that they did not get on a prescription statin. This is proof that no matter what the marketers of these products tell you, "natural" products are not inherently safer than pharmaceutical products.

Green Tea

Green tea has been shown to lower cholesterol in animals, and there are logical reasons why it would help prevent atherosclerosis in humans, including its high level of antioxidants known as flavonoids. But human trials have had mixed results. However, a recent trial published in the *Archives of Internal Medicine* gave some more hope for this traditionally Asian drink. In this study, the 114 Chinese adults who received a pill extract of green tea in addition to sticking to their low-fat diet lowered their cholesterol further than the 106 who ate similarly but took a placebo.

Another study, this one published in *Circulation* in 2004, explains where some of the discrepancies about green tea's effects on heart disease may come from—the timing of the antioxidant treatment. This study on mice found that the antioxidants in green tea provided heart benefits only when given before atherosclerosis was fully established.

Guggul

This extract from a tree native to Asia was used medicinally as early as 600 B.C. to fight obesity and atherosclerosis, among other things. More recently, it's been used in Asia to lower cholesterol, and it's now making its way into the medicine cabinets of Westerners as well. There are few randomized, controlled trials of this substance, and a recent one shows that guggul doesn't live up to its hype. In this 2003 study, 103 American adults with high cholesterol were assigned to take either a placebo, 1,000 mg of guggul extract, or 2,000 mg of the extract, three times a day. Surprisingly, researchers found that the extract actually increased LDL and decreased HDL. Researchers noted that the higher-fat American diet may have made a difference in how guggul worked, because other trials focused on Asians, who typically eat a diet lower in fat.

Chromium

Though I've heard a lot of people say anecdotally that supplements containing the element chromium help lower cholesterol, I've never come across anything that has convinced me. One small study published in 1990 indicated LDL lowering in people who took chromium, and there is some evidence that it can raise HDL levels in people on beta-blockers, but there surely isn't enough evidence to recommend it.

Quercetin

Quercetin is a flavonoid found in onions, red wine, and green tea. There isn't enough information about this supplement to recommend its use for cholesterol lowering. Studies in animals suggested it might help with high cholesterol, but human studies haven't shown any effect.

Soy Lecithin

Although there is a substantial amount of information on the Internet that states that soy lecithin can reduce blood cholesterol levels, there is surprisingly little published scientific information to support that conclusion. I was able to find only a single study in which soy stanol–lecithin powder was reported to reduce cholesterol absorption in the intestine and cause a 14 percent reduction in LDL cholesterol levels. This study indicates that only a specific combination of ingredients was effective for cholesterol lowering. Other nutritional supplements that don't contain the same ingredients as in the one tested might not yield that same benefit.

Garlic

In 2000, researchers did an analysis of the studies published on garlic and cholesterol. They found that garlic generally reduces cholesterol by an average of .41 mmol/L compared to placebo. This lowering isn't impressive when compared to other interventions, such as a healthy diet's impact of a 5 percent decrease. Also, all of the trials did not show that garlic improved cholesterol, and the study authors did not endorse garlic as a means of controlling cholesterol. That said, if you simply like garlic, there's no reason not to add it to your favorite dishes. Note though that high doses of garlic (such as those found in garlic supplements) can decrease the stickiness of platelets, making a person more prone to heavy bleeding. Because aspirin and warfarin (and other drugs) have the same effect, combining garlic with these drugs can cause problems.

Vitamins C and E

Scientists theorized that vitamin E might help fight heart disease in three ways: by preventing the oxidation of LDL cholesterol that contributes to the buildup of plaque on artery walls, by inhibiting the proliferation of smooth muscle cells that narrows blood vessels, and by making platelets less sticky and thus less liable to clot. Yet large-scale studies haven't offered much firm support. Instead, the research on E has lurched back and forth.

The observational Nurses' Health Study and the Health Professionals Follow-Up Study found that vitamin E reduced coronary heart disease risk among people who took daily supplements containing at least 100 IU of vitamin E for two years or more. In randomized trials of people who were at higher risk for heart disease or already had it, however, benefits have not been consistent.

Recommended Daily Allowances

Here are guidelines for the average amount of vitamins C and E needed by almost all healthy people.

Vitamin C

Men age 31 and up	90 mg
Women age 31 and up	75 mg
Smokers	Add 35 mg

Vitamin E

Men and women age 31 and up	15 mg

One of the randomized studies found lower rates of heart attack and death from heart disease among people given 400 IU (equivalent to 268 mg of E from food or 180 mg of synthetic E) or 800 IU of vitamin E rather than a placebo. However, in three other large-scale randomized studies, various doses of vitamin E didn't significantly reduce cardiovascular events. Because many of these studies involved high-risk populations or had other limitations, it's still possible that vitamin E could have protective effects, but I think that hope has faded considerably in the past few years.

This area of research is of particular interest to me because when I was at MIT, my colleagues and I cloned a protein called the scavenger receptor. It was the first molecule identified to bring the oxidized form of LDL into the key inflammatory cell involved in atherosclerosis, the macrophage. So, more than most physicians, I was hoping that antioxidant therapies would be effective because that would mean that the process I have spent much of my research career studying is vitally important in heart disease. But the training of a scientist taught me to discard a hypothesis, even a cherished one, when the facts no longer support it. At the moment, I don't believe we can recommend vitamin E treatments as a way of preventing heart disease. However, vitamin E is safe (except at very high doses), so I do not insist that my patients avoid vitamin E if they believe it is providing them a benefit.

A large study known as the Heart Protection Study also dampened hope that vitamin C might be a magic cholesterol-lowering bullet. Other studies had suggested that antioxidant vitamins such as C might decrease coronary disease risk, among other things. But this study of more than twenty thousand adults with diabetes or coronary or other artery disease said otherwise. Half the people were randomly assigned to receive high-dose supplements of vitamins E, C, and beta-carotene; the other half received a placebo. At the end of five years, a similar number of people in each group had had coronary events, stroke, or death.

Like vitamin E, most studies of vitamin C were done on patients at high risk for heart disease. So what they didn't study was whether or not vitamin C can prevent heart disease. Until those studies are done, I don't suggest that patients get any more of any vitamin than the recommended daily allowance for their gender and age groups.

The Bottom Line

Diet, exercise, and the medications listed in Chapter 8 improve cholesterol profiles. So if you have a problem, you should start with them. If you prefer to try something else, talk to your doctor. Even though you don't need a prescription to get an herbal supplement, they can still interact with other medications, cause side effects, and harm a growing fetus or child. Always talk to your doctor before you start a supplement, and remind him or her that you're still taking it at every appointment.

Afterword

If you've read this far, you should have a pretty good understanding of cholesterol—what it is, why high levels of certain types of cholesterol can cause cardiovascular problems, and, most important, what you can do to prevent or treat those high levels through lifestyle changes, medications, or both. The approaches I have outlined and the patient stories presented are intended to illustrate current strategies you can use to reduce your risk of developing cardiovascular disease.

Many of the topics covered involve taking steps that you can accomplish on your own. Some should only be undertaken after consulting with your physician. The prescription medication choices, of course, require a physician's input. Your doctor may have good medical reasons to recommend a treatment plan that differs from an approach that I have discussed because only your doctor can individualize your treatment to your particular medical needs.

If you have questions or concerns about how your doctor is handling your health, it is worth voicing them at your next appointment. I find that patients who are educated about their health issues and are activate participants in their medical decisions are much more likely to give the effort it takes to adopt a healthier lifestyle and take medicines regularly. Don't be afraid to ask your doctor questions about the treatments prescribed. Doctors are busy people, but they have an obligation to explain the therapies they prescribe in clear and understandable terms. If your doctor seems uncertain about how to treat your situation or is too busy to explain your treatment, it can be helpful to get a second opinion from another specialist. In the lipid field, local endocrinologists or cardiologists are likely to be the best sources of information about treatment.

In almost all regions of the country, there are also academic medical centers where very highly specialized physicians—who often teach and do research in the lipid field, as well as take care of patients—work. These experts are usually delighted to work with your local physician to design an optimal treatment program for you. Finally, the pace of change in the field of medicine is remarkable, so it is important to remember that the information in this book will become out-of-date as time passes.

I hope that this book will help you and your family be smarter warriors in the battle against heart disease. I also hope that it will contribute to your living a long and healthy life, free of anxiety over your cholesterol levels because they are exactly where they ought to be.

Resources

General

American Heart Association (AHA)
7272 Greenville Avenue
Dallas, TX 75231
(800) 242-8721 (or check the Yellow Pages
for your local affiliate)
americanheart.org

Operates a consumer hotline to answer questions on general heart health. Offers educational pamphlets, posters, and audiovisual materials on cholesterol and diet modification, all at no charge or for a nominal fee.

Harvard Heart Letter
P.O. Box 420378
Palm Coast, FL 32141
(800) 829-9171
health.harvard.edu/heart

The *Harvard Heart Letter*, published by Harvard Medical School, is a monthly newsletter that delivers expert advice and authoritative information to people who may already suffer from heart disease, or who are concerned about their risk for it and wish to take steps toward a positive change.

National Cholesterol Education Program (NCEP)
NHLBI Health Information Network
P.O. Box 30105
Bethesda, MD 20824-0105
(301) 592-8573
(800) 575-9355 (consumer hotline with recorded messages)
nhlbi.nih.gov

A program of the National Heart, Lung, and Blood Institute. The National Cholesterol Education Program guidelines are available on this website.

Diabetes Issues

American Diabetes Association (ADA)
Attn: National Call Center
1701 North Beauregard Street
Alexandria, VA 22311
(800) DIABETES (342-2383)
diabetes.org

The American Diabetes Association is a nonprofit health organization providing diabetes research, information, and advocacy. It conducts programs in all fifty states and the District of Columbia. The ADA's mission is to prevent and cure diabetes and to help improve the lives of those affected by the disease.

Smoking Cessation

American Cancer Society
1599 Clifton Road NE
Atlanta, GA 30329
(800) ACS-2345
cancer.org

Offers information and support for smokers who want to quit. Its website provides links to support groups, or you can call for information on a group near you.

American Lung Association
61 Broadway, 6th Floor
New York, NY 10006
(800) LUNG-USA (toll-free)
lungusa.org

Continues to research the latest developments in lung care and has many programs and strategies for fighting lung disease. The *Quit Smoking Action Plan* offers specific recommendations for selecting a personalized three-step plan (preparing to quit, using medications, and staying smoke-free) to free yourself of cigarettes and stay that way.

Saving Money on Drugs

DestinationRx
Destinationrx.com

This website gathers and displays drug prices from several online pharmacies. It also offers a discount card.

National Council on the Aging Benefits CheckUp
P.O. Box 411
Annapolis Junction, MD 20701
(800) 373-4906
benefitscheckup.org

This website helps people age fifty-five and over meet the costs of prescription drugs, health care, utilities, and other essential items or services. It also provides descriptions of money-saving programs, local contacts for additional information, and materials to help successfully apply for each program.

AARP MembeRx Choice Plan
(866) 507-9622
aarppharmacy.com

Peoples Prescription Plan
(800) 566-0003
peoplesrxcard.com

Together Rx Card
(800) 865-7211
together-rx.com

Together Rx provides free prescription savings for qualified Medicare enrollees. The Together Rx card entitles holders to approximately a 20 percent to 40 percent discount at most pharmacies.

United States Pharmaceutical Group
(800) 977-9655
uspgi.com

U.S. Military Tricare Program
(877) 363-6337
tricare.osd.mil/pharmacy

Nutrition

American Dietetic Association
120 South Riverside Plaza
Suite 2000
Chicago, IL 60606-6995
(800) 877-1600
eatright.org

Operates a dietitian referral line. This website features extensive nutrition news and information, plus a dietitian locator.

Harvard School of Public Health Nutrition
www.hsph.harvard.edu/nutritionsource

A useful and up-to-date source of dietary information.

Eat, Drink, and Be Healthy
Walter C. Willett, M.D., with P. J. Skerrett. New York:
Harvard Health Publications and Simon and Schuster, 2005.

Based on the latest nutritional science, this easy-to-understand book explains the connection between diet and disease and spells out a practical approach to healthy eating.

The Healthy Heart Cookbook
Joseph C. Piscatella and Bernie Piscatella. New York: Black Dog and Leventhal Publishers, 2004.

This cookbook contains more than seven hundred recipes that cover everything from soups to desserts.

Index